GoodHousekeeping

FAST WEEKNIGHT
FAVORITES!

SIMPLY DELICIOUS MEALS IN 30 MINUTES OR LESS

Roasted Salmon with Summer Squash (page 98)

Good Housekeeping

FAST WEEKNIGHT
FAVORITES!

SIMPLY DELICIOUS MEALS IN 30 MINUTES OR LESS

HEARST BOOKS

A division of Sterling Publishing Co., Inc.

New York / London

www.sterlingpublishing.com

GOOD HOUSEKEEPING

Rosemary Ellis
EDITOR IN CHIEF

Sara Lyle
LIFESTYLE EDITOR

Susan Westmoreland
FOOD DIRECTOR

Samantha B. Cassetty, M.S., R.D.
NUTRITION DIRECTOR

Sharon Franke
FOOD APPLIANCES DIRECTOR

BOOK DESIGN by Memo Productions
PROJECT EDITOR Sarah Scheffel
Photography Credits on page 158

Library of Congress
Cataloging-in-Publication Data is available.

10 9 8 7 6 5 4 3 2 1

Published by Hearst Books
A division of Sterling Publishing Co., Inc.
387 Park Avenue South, New York, NY 10016

Good Housekeeping is a registered trademark of Hearst Communications, Inc.

www.goodhousekeeping.com

For information about custom editions, special sales, premium and corporate purchases, please contact Sterling Special Sales Department at 800-805-5489 or specialsales@sterlingpublishing.com.

Distributed in Canada by Sterling Publishing
c/o Canadian Manda Group, 165 Dufferin Street
Toronto, Ontario, Canada M6K 3H6

Distributed in Australia by Capricorn Link
(Australia) Pty. Ltd.
P.O. Box 704, Windsor, NSW 2756 Australia

Manufactured in China

Sterling ISBN 978-1-58816-877-1

CONTENTS

Pork Tenderloin with Roasted Grapes (page 78)

FOREWORD

Like you, we in the *Good Housekeeping* food department often wonder how to feed our families at the end of an action-packed day. *Fast Weeknight Favorites* is our answer to that dilemma. You don't have to serve takeout food or fuss frantically in the kitchen to get dinner ready. Instead, with this cookbook as your kitchen companion, you can have a healthy, home-cooked meal ready in thirty minutes or less.

We've compiled these fast and easy recipes to give you plenty of hassle-free weeknight options. There are delicious main dishes made with meat, fish, shellfish, poultry, and pasta, as well as tasty vegetarian selections. Try our Sweet and Tangy Braised Chuck Roast, Teriyaki Salmon with Gingery Chard, Zucchini and Bean Burritos, or Low 'n' Slow Pulled Pork (toss ingredients in your slow cooker in the a.m. and you'll have a satisfying meal in the p.m.). **Icons indicate the quick-cooking methods employed in each recipe.**

STOVE   OVEN   MICRO WAVE   GRILL   SLOW   NO COOK

We hope all of the dishes in *Fast Weeknight Favorites* will get raves from your family, and help you transform dinnertime from a harried ordeal in the kitchen into a relaxed family experience. But express cooking is only one facet of *Fast Weeknight Favorites*. Planning, shopping, and organizing efficiently are the others. (Many dishes make use of convenience foods and pantry staples, from rotisserie chicken to bottled condiments to frozen veggies.) Be sure to read the introduction for lots of great *Good Housekeeping* advice on ways to save time even before you begin to cook.

SUSAN WESTMORELAND
Food Director, *Good Housekeeping*

SUPER SUPPERS—FAST

It's the end of a busy day, you're running late, and there are still tons of things to do before you head home to start dinner. How are you ever going to put supper on the table? Trust us, preparing a meal for your family that is quick, healthy, and delicious is not an unattainable goal. *Fast Weeknight Favorites* has dozens of mouthwatering recipes for homemade dinners that can be prepped and cooked in thirty minutes or less with ease—without sacrificing valued time with your family.

PLAN AHEAD

Keep it simple. Choose dishes with a limited number of ingredients that use simple cooking techniques. The aim is to spend dinnertime with your family, not to be bustling in the kitchen.

Make a shopping list. Put aside some time once a week to plan menu ideas for the days ahead. Read the recipes you want to cook, taking note of all ingredients called for. Check your pantry, your freezer, and your refrigerator to see what you already have. Then plan your shopping list accordingly and keep it updated by adding other items as you think of them.

Shop and stock up. With shopping list in hand, navigate the supermarket for staples, sale items, and all the components you'll need for the week's menus. Doing a "big" shopping trip once a week and limiting or eliminating midweek trips to the market is a simple yet effective time and money saver. Once you get home, be sure to wrap, pack, and store perishables properly to avoid waste. To get the job done quickly, enlist your family members to help with the unpacking.

Cook ahead. Weekends are great times for making large batches of soups, stews, or casseroles. Serve some right away and freeze the rest for another day. If you can, prepare a few basic foods that can be incorporated into meals during the week ahead: cook up a pot of rice or other grain, make pasta sauce, roast potatoes, butternut squash, or a mix of seasonal vegetables.

SHOP SMART, SHOP QUICKLY

Most supermarkets are arranged in a similar manner. Produce is in the front of the store; meats, dairy, deli, baked goods, and frozen items are usually around the perimeter, while the aisles are stocked with bottled, canned, and packaged goods. Arrange your shopping list by grocery departments and use it as a map to your local market. You'll know exactly where to find everything you need and won't waste time browsing. Start with the staples, move on to the perishables, then the refrigerated items. Save frozen foods for last so they'll stay cold; they'll also help cool your perishable and refrigerated groceries.

PREPPED AND PREMADE FOODS

Supermarkets carry a vast selection of foods that are available already prepared or prepped. These items make feeding a hungry family on busy weeknights a breeze.

• Items such as rotisserie chicken, chili, soups, pasta dishes, and pot pies, as well as choices from the salad bar, can form the basis of hearty no-cook dinners.

• Cleaned and ready to use, sliced, diced, and shredded fresh vegetables can be found in the produce section along with packaged, peeled, and sliced fresh fruits.

• Packaged salad greens come cut, washed, and mixed with other veggies to go straight from the bag to the salad bowl. Just be sure to check the packaging to make sure it says *washed* and *ready-to-eat*, as some bagged salad greens must be rinsed before eating.

• Frozen vegetables—available in a variety of styles and combinations, including ethnic mixes like Asian and Mediterranean—aren't just for side dishes. They can be tossed into stir-fries and pasta dishes.

• Meats, fish, and poultry are sold seasoned and marinated, even prepared as kabobs or stuffed rolls. All you provide is the grilling, roasting, steaming, stir-frying, or sautéing.

• Precooked and packaged chicken pieces, meatballs, and flavored sausages (or, for a vegetarian meal, preseasoned tofu or tempeh) can help you get dinner on the table in a flash.

SHOPPING SHORTCUTS

Strategic shopping makes weeknight cooking fast and easy. Keep these tips in mind as you push your cart through the aisles. And remember, it always pays to shop with a list in hand; see Plan Ahead on page 8 for list-making pointers.

• Stock up when there's a sale on meats, poultry, seafood, or frozen foods you use. For meats, poultry, and seafood, separate what you plan to cook within two days, then wrap the rest in meal-size portions and freeze them immediately.

• Choose items that cook up fast. Use chicken tenders instead of whole chicken pieces and thinly sliced medallions of pork instead of thick loin chops; select vegetables that have been cut into matchstick-size pieces, which cook evenly and more quickly than whole veggies or large chunks.

• Take advantage of convenience products that are nutritious and have the fewest preservatives and artificial ingredients. Some options include whole-wheat tortilla wraps and pre- or partially baked pizza shells, quick-cooking rice or whole-grain pilafs, rotisserie chicken, preshredded cabbage or broccoli slaw, prewashed salad greens, and peeled, chopped fruit and veggies (fresh or frozen).

• Think outside the box—or bottle or package. Spice blends in any of a variety of flavors can be mixed into ground beef to give meatballs, burgers, or meat loaf an exotic twist. Bottled creamy salad dressings can top mashed or baked potatoes instead of butter or sour cream; you can sauté fresh vegetables with a tablespoon of vinaigrette dressing instead of oil. Garlic-flavored spreadable cheese thinned with a little milk makes a delectable sauce for pasta or vegetables.

STOCK UP

Do you often have a good idea for a quick weeknight meal only to discover that you have to stop at the grocery store first in order to pick up a few essential ingredients? Keeping your kitchen stocked with foods you use on a regular basis will not only cut down on your shopping and prepping time, it will ensure that no matter how busy you are, you'll always have the makings of a healthy meal.

PANTRY (NONPERISHABLES AND NONREFRIGERATED LONG-LASTING ITEMS)

Every week or so, check your larder and add any items that are running low to your shopping list. Here are some long-lasting items that are great to have on hand, although the list will of course vary from household to household, depending on the tastes and habits of its residents.

- Quick-cooking white and brown rice, couscous, and other quick-cooking grains
- Flavored rice mixes
- A variety of pasta shapes
- Canned broths and soups, packaged soup mixes
- Canned tomato products: crushed, diced, and sauce
- Canned tuna and salmon
- Canned and dried fruit
- Nuts, peanut butter or other nut butters (check the label to see if refrigeration is required once opened)
- Oils: shelf-stable extra-virgin and light olive oils, sesame oil, and a nut oil (check the label to see if the nut oil should be refrigerated)
- Dried herbs and spices (alone and in blends)
- Condiments: vinegars, relishes, pickles, chutneys, mustards, ketchup, olives, sun-dried tomatoes, pesto, salsas (check the label to see if refrigeration is required once opened)
- Salad dressings and bottled sauces such as steak, soy, peanut, and curry (check the label to see if refrigeration is required once opened)
- Sweeteners: sugar or sugar substitute, honey, jams (refrigerate jams once opened)
- Baking staples: flour, baking powder and soda, brown sugar and confectioners' sugar, vanilla extract, baker's chocolate and chocolate chips
- Potatoes, onions, garlic, shallots
- Boxed cereal and quick-cooking oatmeal (the flavored serving-sized packets are handy)
- Tortilla chips, salad croutons, saltines and other favorite crackers
- Tea, hot chocolate mix, coffee (beans, ground, or instant, according to your preferences)

REFRIGERATOR

Place items that are used most often in the front of the fridge and lesser-used items behind them. Take note of the rear items you have in stock about every other week, so you remember to use them.

- Fresh meats, fish, and poultry
- Fresh vegetables (whole and chopped) and greens
- Fresh pasta (cooks faster than dried)
- Sliced deli meats, whole sausages, bacon, tofu
- Cheeses: sliced deli cheeses, feta, blue, freshly grated Parmesan, and Cheddar
- Milk, yogurt, and sour cream
- Butter and cream cheese
- Mayonnaise
- Citrus fruits
- Juices and other beverages

FREEZER

Wrap meat and poultry in freezer wrap or heavy-duty foil, pressing out all the air.

Label each package with the name of the cut, the number of servings, and the date. To freeze seafood, be sure it is very fresh, and wrap it in both plastic wrap and heavy-duty foil. Always freeze foods in meal-sized or recipe-sized portions unless it will be a simple matter to remove the amount you need from the frozen package.

- Fresh meat, fish, and poultry to be used at a later date
- Raw vegetables chopped and prepared for cooking: onions, carrots, bell peppers, celery, leeks, broccoli, and cauliflower florets
- Packaged frozen vegetables and vegetable combos
- Flash-frozen fruits and berries
- Breads, tortillas, pita pockets
- Leftovers—casseroles, soups, stews, grilled meats, and veggies
- Cooked rice and pasta
- Homemade chicken or vegetable broth (freeze in ice cube trays)
- Sliced pound cake (to top with fruit or berries, ice cream, or puddings for a quick dessert)

HOW LONG WILL IT KEEP FROZEN?

Foods frozen for longer than the recommended times aren't harmful—they just won't be at their peak flavor and texture.

FOOD	TIME IN FREEZER (0°F)
Milk	3 months
Butter	6 to 9 months
Cheese, hard (Cheddar, Swiss)	6 months
Cheese, soft (Brie, Bel Paese)	6 months
Cream, half-and-half	4 months
Eggs (raw yolks or whites)	1 year
Frankfurters	1 to 2 months
Luncheon meats	1 to 2 months
Bacon	1 month
Sausage, raw (links or patties)	1 to 2 months
Ham, fully cooked (whole, half, slices)	1 to 2 months
Ground or stew meat	3 to 4 months
Steaks	6 to 12 months
Chops	3 to 6 months
Roasts	4 to 12 months
Chicken or turkey, whole	1 year
Chicken or turkey, pieces	9 months
Casseroles, cooked, poultry	4 to 6 months
Casseroles, cooked, meat	2 to 3 months
Soups and stews	2 to 3 months
Fish, raw, lean (cod, flounder, haddock)	6 months
Fish, raw, fatty (bluefish, mackerel, salmon)	2 to 3 months
Fish, cooked	4 to 6 months
Fish, smoked (in vacuum pack)	2 months
Shrimp, scallops, squid, shucked clams, mussels, oysters	3 to 6 months
Pizza	1 to 2 months
Breads and rolls, yeast	3 to 6 months
Breads, quick	2 to 3 months
Cakes, unfrosted	3 months
Cheesecakes	2 to 3 months
Cookies, baked	3 months
Cookie dough, raw	2 to 3 months
Pies, fruit, unbaked	8 months
Piecrust, raw	2 to 3 months

CUT DOWN KITCHEN TIME

Spend a minute or two to organize your work area and have the appropriate tools and cookware at the ready to speed your preparations along. Get the kids to help out by setting the table, pouring milk, and doing other simple tasks to save you time.

GET ORGANIZED
- Become familiar with your chosen recipe so you don't have to stop to read each step while you work.
- Clear an adequate workspace with plenty of elbow room.
- Assemble all ingredients, cookware, and tools so that everything is within easy reach.
- Set utensils aside after using them; clutter will slow you down.

USEFUL UTENSILS
- Knives: a paring knife for trimming veggies and fruits, a chef's knife for fast slicing and chopping, and a serrated knife to cut through delicate foods like bread, tomatoes, and cake
- A heavy 12-inch nonstick skillet with lid for browning, sautéing, stir-frying, and making sauces
- Heatproof silicone spatulas in a few sizes
- Kitchen scissors for snipping fresh herbs
- A microplane grater for grating hard cheeses, citrus peels, and ginger

TIME-SAVING APPLIANCES

- Mini food processor with changeable cutting disks for chopping, slicing, and shredding
- Immersion blender for pureeing soups and making gravies, dips, and sauces
- Microwave oven for defrosting frozen meats, fish, and poultry; pre-cooking ingredients that take a long time to cook, such as potatoes and winter squash; reheating leftovers; steaming vegetables; melting butter and cheese
- Grill pan (uses very little oil, preheats fast, and leaves the familiar grill marks on the food)
- Toaster oven for quick cheese quesadillas or crusty garlic bread
- Slow cooker (lets you prep, set, and forget—then enjoy a hot home-made dinner at the end of a long day)

SHORTCUTS TO MEAL PREPARATION

- Choose lean cuts of meat, such as sirloin, which will cook faster than fattier cuts, such as chuck. Save tougher cuts for the slow cooker.
- Put water on to boil for pasta or rice, or preheat the oven, as soon as you get home. While the heating begins, you can gather your ingredients, brown meat, or sauté onions, according to the recipe's requirements.
- If you are using ground beef in a recipe, brown it the previous evening, then let it cool, bag it, and refrigerate.
- Boneless, skinless chicken breasts are the basis for so many quick and easy meals. Brush on some barbecue sauce and toss them into a hot grill pan, or slice them and stir-fry with bottled sauce and frozen mixed veggies.
- Cook enough for two or three meals and turn the leftovers into different dishes later in the week. For example, the leftovers from a pot of chili can be used to make tacos and nachos—or as a great baked potato topping.
- Freeze leftovers in individual servings, and you'll have a stockpile of quick and healthy meals whenever you want.
- Incorporate restaurant leftovers into fast and easy meals: extra white rice becomes quick fried rice, leftover pasta with marinara sauce can be tossed with sautéed sausage or chicken pieces.

Chicken Tagine (page 23)

TOP 10 SLOW-COOKER TIPS

The slow cooker is a brilliant time-saving device, perfect for preparing many simple meals like the Chicken Tagine pictured opposite.

1 Prep the recipe the night before: measure ingredients, cut vegetables, trim meats, mix liquids and seasonings. Refrigerate the components separately in zip-tight plastic bags or containers. In the morning, place them in the cooker, turn it on, and go about your day.

2 Cut meats and vegetables for soups and stews into uniform, bite-size pieces to ensure even cooking.

3 Start with the crock at room temperature. Don't use frozen ingredients, which prolong the heating process, increasing the risk that harmful bacteria may survive. Thaw meats, poultry, and veggies before adding them to the slow cooker.

4 For richer flavor, dredge meats and poultry in flour and brown the pieces in a nonstick skillet before adding them to the slow cooker. Scrape up the browned bits and add them to the cooker for a heartier sauce.

5 Use assertive spices and seasonings such as chili powder and garlic sparingly, as slow cooking tends to intensify these flavors. Dried herbs may lose some of their flavor, so adjust the seasonings at the end of the cooking time. If you are using fresh herbs, save some to add at the last minute.

6 Add dairy products such as milk or yogurt during the last hour of cooking to prevent curdling, or use canned evaporated milk.

7 For even cooking, fill the slow cooker at least halfway, but never to the brim. Place hard vegetables like turnips and potatoes on the bottom; they cook more slowly than meat. For soups and stews, leave about 2 inches of space below the rim.

8 Always cook covered. Lift the lid as little as possible during the cooking process—it allows steam to escape and reduces the internal temperature. Stirring is usually not necessary; the flavors blend automatically as the steam that builds in the pot penetrates the cooking food. Add twenty minutes to the cooking time whenever you lift the lid.

9 If your recipe yields more liquid than you want, transfer the solids to a serving dish and keep them warm. Turn the slow cooker to High and cook the remaining liquid until it is reduced to the desired thickness.

10 To convert a regular recipe, use about half the liquid called for and add more during the last hour of cooking, if needed.

CHICKEN & TURKEY

Double-Dipped Potato-Chip Chicken with Quick Slaw (page 42)

WARM CHICKEN SALAD WITH MUSTARD-THYME VINAIGRETTE

STOVE This hearty salad is dressed with a tangy vinaigrette that contains Dijon mustard with seeds. Dijon, like most European mustards, is made from brown seeds and is much zestier and more flavorful than American-style prepared mustard. You can substitute other mustards, but you won't get the same bold flavor.

ACTIVE TIME: 20 MINUTES

MAKES: 4 SERVINGS

3   SLICES BACON, EACH CUT INTO ½-INCH PIECES

3   GREEN ONIONS, THINLY SLICED

⅓   CUP CIDER VINEGAR OR RED WINE VINEGAR

1   TABLESPOON OLIVE OIL

1   TABLESPOON DIJON MUSTARD WITH SEEDS

2   TEASPOONS FRESH THYME LEAVES

½   TEASPOON SALT

3   CUPS (15 OUNCES) COARSELY SHREDDED SKINLESS ROTISSERIE CHICKEN MEAT

1   RED DELICIOUS, GALA, OR FUJI APPLE, NOT PEELED, CORED AND THINLY SLICED

1   BAG (5 TO 6 OUNCES) PREWASHED BABY SPINACH

1   In nonstick 10-inch skillet, cook bacon over medium heat, stirring occasionally, until browned, 5 to 6 minutes. Add green onions and cook, 1 minute. Remove skillet from heat. Stir in vinegar, oil, mustard, thyme, and salt.

2   Meanwhile, in large serving bowl, toss chicken with apple and spinach until combined.

3   Pour hot dressing over chicken mixture; toss until salad is evenly coated. Serve immediately.

EACH SERVING: ABOUT 385 CALORIES | 29G PROTEIN | 8G CARBOHYDRATE | 27G TOTAL FAT (8G SATURATED) | 5G FIBER | 95MG CHOLESTEROL | 675MG SODIUM

CHICKEN WITH BLACK BEANS AND SWEET POTATOES

 This spicy, smoky slow-cooker meal takes only about fifteen minutes to prep, so it is easy to throw together in the morning.

ACTIVE TIME: 15 MINUTES · SLOW-COOK: 8 HOURS ON LOW OR 4 HOURS ON HIGH
MAKES: 6 SERVINGS

3 POUNDS BONE-IN CHICKEN THIGHS, SKIN AND FAT REMOVED

2 TEASPOONS GROUND CUMIN

¼ TEASPOON SALT

¼ TEASPOON GROUND BLACK PEPPER

1 TEASPOON SMOKED PAPRIKA OR ½ TEASPOON CHOPPED CHIPOTLE CHILES IN ADOBO SAUCE

½ TEASPOON GROUND ALLSPICE

1 CUP REDUCED-SODIUM CHICKEN BROTH

½ CUP SALSA

3 LARGE GARLIC CLOVES, CRUSHED WITH GARLIC PRESS

2 CANS (15 TO 19 OUNCES EACH) BLACK BEANS, RINSED AND DRAINED

2 POUNDS SWEET POTATOES, PEELED AND CUT INTO 2-INCH PIECES

1 TO 2 ROASTED RED PEPPERS FROM JAR, CUT INTO STRIPS (1 CUP)

⅓ CUP LOOSELY PACKED FRESH CILANTRO LEAVES, CHOPPED

LIME WEDGES

1 Sprinkle chicken thighs with ½ teaspoon ground cumin and salt and pepper. Heat 12-inch nonstick skillet over medium heat until hot. Add chicken and cook until well browned on all sides, about 10 minutes. With tongs, transfer chicken to plate. Remove skillet from heat.

2 In same skillet, combine smoked paprika, allspice, broth, salsa, garlic, and remaining 1½ teaspoons cumin.

3 In 6-quart slow cooker, combine beans and sweet potatoes. Arrange chicken thighs in single layer on top of sweet-potato mixture; pour broth mixture over chicken. Cover slow cooker and cook as manufacturer directs, 8 hours on Low or 4 hours on High.

4 With tongs or slotted spoon, transfer chicken thighs to large platter. Gently stir roasted red pepper strips into potato mixture; spoon mixture over chicken. Sprinkle with cilantro and serve with lime wedges.

EACH SERVING: ABOUT 415 CALORIES | 36G PROTEIN | 61G CARBOHYDRATE | 6G TOTAL FAT (1G SATURATED) | 12G FIBER | 107MG CHOLESTEROL | 875MG SODIUM

CHICKEN TAGINE

SLOW A tagine is a Moroccan stew of meat or poultry served over couscous. The traditional tagine pot is made of clay; it has a flat bowl for a base and a conical top. A slow cooker, while less spectacular to look at, does a fine job of cooking the dish. For photo, see page 16.

ACTIVE TIME: 20 MINUTES · SLOW-COOK: 8 HOURS ON LOW OR 4 HOURS ON HIGH

MAKES: 6 SERVINGS

1   MEDIUM BUTTERNUT SQUASH (1½ POUNDS), PEELED AND CUT INTO 2-INCH PIECES (SEE TIP)

2   MEDIUM TOMATOES (6 TO 8 OUNCES EACH), COARSELY CHOPPED

1   MEDIUM ONION, CHOPPED

2   GARLIC CLOVES, CRUSHED WITH GARLIC PRESS

1   CAN (15 TO 19 OUNCES) GARBANZO BEANS, RINSED AND DRAINED

1   CUP REDUCED-SODIUM CHICKEN BROTH

⅓   CUP RAISINS

2   TEASPOONS GROUND CORIANDER

2   TEASPOONS GROUND CUMIN

½   TEASPOON GROUND CINNAMON

½   TEASPOON SALT

¼   TEASPOON GROUND BLACK PEPPER

3   POUNDS BONE-IN CHICKEN THIGHS, SKIN AND FAT REMOVED

1   BOX (10 OUNCES) PLAIN COUSCOUS (MOROCCAN PASTA)

½   CUP PITTED GREEN OLIVES

1   In 6-quart slow cooker, combine squash, tomatoes, onion, garlic, beans, broth, and raisins. In cup, combine coriander, cumin, cinnamon, salt, and pepper. Rub spice mixture over chicken thighs. Arrange chicken thighs on top of vegetable mixture. Cover slow cooker and cook as manufacturer directs, 8 hours on Low or 4 hours on High.

2   About 10 minutes before serving, prepare couscous as label directs. Fluff with fork.

3   Gently stir olives into tagine. Serve over couscous.

TIP The best way to peel butternut squash is to cut it into smaller pieces first. Holding it firmly on its side and using a sharp knife, cut it crosswise into 2-inch-thick rounds. Place each round flat side down, and cut away the peel. Then scoop out the seeds and cut as desired. To save time and effort, use a package of peeled, precut butternut squash (available in the produce section of many supermarkets).

EACH SERVING: ABOUT 545 CALORIES | 39G PROTEIN | 80G CARBOHYDRATE | 9G TOTAL FAT (2G SATURATED) | 10G FIBER | 107MG CHOLESTEROL | 855MG SODIUM

EASY COBB SALAD

NO COOK This hearty Cobb salad can be thrown together in just minutes, thanks to ready-cooked bacon and chicken. If you're a traditionalist and have the time, you might want to add a strip of chopped ripe avocado to this popular salad. Since avocado discolors quickly, cut and chop it just before serving or sprinkle the exposed flesh with lemon or lime juice.

TOTAL TIME: 25 MINUTES

MAKES: 6 SERVINGS

---

2   BAGS (5 OUNCES EACH) MIXED BABY GREENS

1   PINT RED OR YELLOW CHERRY OR GRAPE TOMATOES, HALVED

2   CUPS CORN KERNELS CUT FROM COBS (4 EARS)

2   CUPS (10 OUNCES) SKINLESS ROTISSERIE CHICKEN MEAT, CUT INTO ½-INCH CUBES

½   SEEDLESS CUCUMBER, NOT PEELED, FINELY CHOPPED

3   OUNCES BLUE CHEESE, CRUMBLED (¾ CUP)

6   SLICES READY-TO-SERVE BACON, PREPARED AS LABEL DIRECTS, COOLED AND COARSELY CHOPPED

BOTTLED VINAIGRETTE SALAD DRESSING

Line deep, large platter with baby greens. Arrange cherry tomatoes, corn, chicken, cucumber, blue cheese, and bacon in striped pattern over greens. Serve with dressing.

EACH SERVING WITHOUT DRESSING: ABOUT 215 CALORIES | 21G PROTEIN | 16G CARBOHY-DRATE | 3G FIBER | 10G TOTAL FAT (4G SATURATED) | 49MG CHOLESTEROL | 655MG SODIUM

4 IDEAS FOR...
ROTISSERIE CHICKEN

The succulent meat from a supermarket rotisserie chicken forms a tasty base for quick, healthy meals.

Mediterranean Chicken Pasta: In a large skillet coated with cooking spray, add 2 cups chopped marinated artichoke hearts, 1 cup chopped tomatoes, 4 tablespoons chopped Kalamata olives, and 4 cups chopped skinless, boneless white breast meat (or 3 cups dark meat) from a rotisserie chicken and cook until warmed through. Serve over 4 cups cooked penne and top with ¼ cup feta cheese and ½ cup chopped basil. Season with ground black pepper and a sprinkle of salt. Makes 4 servings.

Chicken Waldorf Salad: Combine 6 cups broccoli slaw, 4 cups chopped Granny Smith apples (about 4 small), 1 cup halved seedless grapes, ¼ cup chopped walnuts, ¼ cup crumbled blue cheese, and 4 cups chopped or shredded skinless, boneless white breast meat (or 3 cups dark meat) from a rotisserie chicken. Stir in ¾ cup plain yogurt, ¼ cup lemon juice, and ½ teaspoon ground black pepper. Serve salad over 8 cups mixed greens. Makes 4 servings.

Caribbean Chicken Wrap: Combine 2 cups chopped or shredded skinless, boneless white breast meat (or 1½ cups dark meat) from a rotisserie chicken with ½ cup chopped red onion, 8 chopped garlic cloves, 2 cups cubed mango, 1 cup drained and rinsed canned black beans, a pinch of red pepper flakes, and 3 tablespoons chopped cilantro. Divide filling between 4 wheat tortillas and roll up. Makes 4 wraps.

Chicken and Cannellini Couscous: Combine 2½ cups cooked couscous with 2 cups rinsed and drained canned cannellini beans, 1 cup chopped red onion, 2 cups halved grape tomatoes, 1 cup marinated artichoke hearts, and 2 cups chopped or shredded skinless, boneless white breast meat (or 1½ cups dark meat) from a rotisserie chicken. Drizzle with ¾ cup lemon juice, 4 teaspoons olive oil, ½ cup chopped fresh basil, and ¼ cup crumbled feta cheese. Season with ground black pepper and a sprinkling of sea salt. Makes 4 servings.

CHICKEN STIR-FRY WITH CABBAGE

 STOVE **This fast, healthful stir-fry showcases succulent chunks of chicken and tender-crisp vegetables in a mild ginger sauce.**

TOTAL TIME: 30 MINUTES

MAKES: 4 SERVINGS

1   CUP LONG-GRAIN WHITE RICE

1   TABLESPOON VEGETABLE OIL

1   GARLIC CLOVE, CRUSHED WITH GARLIC PRESS

1   POUND SKINLESS, BONELESS CHICKEN THIGHS, CUT INTO 1-INCH PIECES

3   GREEN ONIONS, CUT INTO 1½-INCH PIECES

1   MEDIUM RED PEPPER, THINLY SLICED

½   SMALL HEAD GREEN CABBAGE, CUT INTO 1-INCH PIECES (ABOUT 4 CUPS; SEE TIP)

1   CUP REDUCED-SODIUM CHICKEN BROTH

2   TABLESPOONS REDUCED-SODIUM SOY SAUCE

1   TABLESPOON CORNSTARCH

2   TEASPOONS GRATED, PEELED FRESH GINGER

1   Prepare rice as label directs.

2   Meanwhile, in 12-inch nonstick skillet, heat oil and garlic over medium heat until hot. Add chicken and green onions and cook, stirring frequently (stir-frying), until chicken is well browned and loses its pink color through-out, 5 to 6 minutes. With slotted spoon, transfer mixture to medium bowl.

3   To same skillet, add red pepper, cabbage, and ¼ cup broth; stir to com-bine. Cover and cook over medium heat, stirring occasionally, until veg-etables are tender-crisp, about 5 minutes. Transfer to bowl with chicken.

4   Meanwhile, in cup, stir soy sauce, cornstarch, ginger, and remaining ¾ cup broth until blended and smooth. Add mixture to skillet and heat to boiling over high heat; boil 1 minute. Remove skillet from heat. Stir chicken and vegetables into broth mixture; heat through. Serve with rice.

TIP Preparing the cabbage for this crunchy stir-fry is a snap. All you do is slice the head in half (or in fourths, if the cabbage is large) and, holding each piece firmly, cut away the core. After discarding the core, turn each piece flat side down and cut it to the desired size. Wrap the unused portion of the cabbage tightly in plastic and refrigerate. Use within two days.

EACH SERVING: ABOUT 385 CALORIES | 29G PROTEIN | 48G CARBOHYDRATE | 9G TOTAL FAT (2G SATURATED) | 3G FIBER | 94MG CHOLESTEROL | 525MG SODIUM

JAMAICAN JERK CHICKEN KABOBS

GRILL Originally, jerk seasoning was only used to season pork shoulder, which was "jerked" apart into shreds before serving. Nowadays, this very popular power-packed seasoning rub is enjoyed on fish and chicken as well.

ACTIVE TIME: 15 MINUTES PLUS MARINATING · **TOTAL TIME:** 25 MINUTES
MAKES: 4 SERVINGS

2	GREEN ONIONS, CHOPPED	1	TEASPOON DRIED THYME
1	JALAPEÑO CHILE, SEEDED AND MINCED	½	TEASPOON PLUS ⅛ TEASPOON SALT
1	TABLESPOON MINCED, PEELED FRESH GINGER	1	POUND SKINLESS, BONELESS CHICKEN BREAST HALVES, CUT INTO 12 PIECES
2	TABLESPOONS WHITE WINE VINEGAR	1	RED PEPPER, STEM AND SEEDS REMOVED, CUT INTO 1-INCH PIECES
2	TABLESPOONS WORCESTERSHIRE SAUCE	1	GREEN PEPPER, STEM AND SEEDS REMOVED, CUT INTO 1-INCH PIECES
3	TEASPOONS VEGETABLE OIL	4	(10-INCH) METAL SKEWERS
1	TEASPOON GROUND ALLSPICE		

1 In blender or in food processor with knife blade attached, process green onions, jalapeño, ginger, vinegar, Worcestershire, 2 teaspoons oil, allspice, thyme, and ½ teaspoon salt until paste forms.

2 Place chicken in small bowl or ziptight plastic bag and add green-onion mixture, turning to coat chicken. Cover bowl or seal bag and refrigerate 1 hour to marinate.

3 Meanwhile, in small bowl, toss red and green peppers with remaining 1 teaspoon oil and remaining ⅛ teaspoon salt.

4 Prepare outdoor grill for direct grilling over medium heat. Alternately thread chicken and pepper pieces on each skewer.

5 Place kabobs on hot grill rack over medium heat. Brush kabobs with any remaining marinade. Cook kabobs 5 minutes; turn and cook until chicken loses its pink color throughout, about 5 minutes longer.

EACH SERVING: ABOUT 180 CALORIES | 27G PROTEIN | 6G CARBOHYDRATE | 5G TOTAL FAT (1G SATURATED) | 2G FIBER | 66MG CHOLESTEROL | 525MG SODIUM

SKILLET CHICKEN PARMESAN

 Chicken stands in for the usual breaded, fried, and baked eggplant in this quick stovetop version of the Italian classic. For extra kick, try using Bel Paese or Fontina cheese in place of the mozzarella.

TOTAL TIME: 20 MINUTES

MAKES: 4 SERVINGS

1 TEASPOON OLIVE OIL	2 PLUM TOMATOES, CHOPPED
1 POUND THINLY SLICED CHICKEN BREAST CUTLETS	2 TABLESPOONS FRESHLY GRATED PARMESAN CHEESE
1 CONTAINER (15 OUNCES) REFRIGERATED MARINARA SAUCE	1 CUP LOOSELY PACKED FRESH BASIL LEAVES, SLICED
4 OUNCES PART-SKIM MOZZARELLA CHEESE, SHREDDED (1 CUP)	

1   In nonstick 12-inch skillet, heat oil over medium heat until hot. Add half of chicken breasts to skillet and cook, turning once, until chicken just loses its pink color throughout, about 5 minutes. With tongs, transfer cooked chicken to plate; repeat with remaining cutlets.

2   Return chicken breasts to skillet over medium heat; top with marinara sauce and mozzarella. Cover and cook until sauce is heated through and mozzarella has melted, 2 minutes. To serve, sprinkle with tomatoes, Parmesan, and basil.

EACH SERVING: ABOUT 295 CALORIES | 36G PROTEIN | 10G CARBOHYDRATE | 11G TOTAL FAT (4G SATURATED) | 2G FIBER | 84MG CHOLESTEROL | 660MG SODIUM

QUICK CHICKEN MOLE

STOVE Our speedy version of mole, a richly flavored sauce with spices, peanut butter, and raisins, is authentic enough to satisfy any Mexican-food aficionado. For a quick side salad, serve with packaged prewashed and torn romaine leaves and thin slices of ripe avocado.

TOTAL TIME: 25 MINUTES

MAKES: 4 SERVINGS

2	TEASPOONS OLIVE OIL	1	TABLESPOON TOMATO PASTE
1	MEDIUM ONION, CHOPPED	¼	CUP GOLDEN OR DARK RAISINS
2	GARLIC CLOVES, CRUSHED WITH GARLIC PRESS	1	ROTISSERIE CHICKEN (2 TO 2½ POUNDS), CUT INTO 8 PIECES, SKIN REMOVED, IF YOU LIKE
2	TEASPOONS CHILI POWDER		
2	TEASPOONS UNSWEETENED COCOA	¼	CUP LOOSELY PACKED FRESH CILANTRO LEAVES, CHOPPED
¼	TEASPOON GROUND CINNAMON		COOKED RICE (OPTIONAL)
1¼	CUPS CHICKEN BROTH		ROMAINE AND AVOCADO SALAD (OPTIONAL)
1	TABLESPOON CREAMY PEANUT BUTTER		LIME WEDGES

1 In nonstick 12-inch skillet, heat oil over medium heat until hot. Add onion and cook, stirring occasionally, 5 minutes. Add garlic, chili powder, cocoa, and cinnamon to skillet; cook, stirring constantly, 1 minute.

2 Stir in broth, peanut butter, and tomato paste. Add raisins; heat to boiling. Add chicken pieces to skillet. Reduce heat to medium-low; cover and simmer about 5 minutes, turning chicken pieces halfway through cooking to coat all sides with sauce (cook 10 minutes if chicken has been refrigerated).

3 Sprinkle chicken with cilantro. Serve chicken and sauce over rice with salad, if you like. Garnish with lime wedges.

EACH SERVING WITHOUT SKIN: ABOUT 400 CALORIES | 44G PROTEIN | 15G CARBOHYDRATE 18G TOTAL FAT (4G SATURATED) | 3G FIBER | 126MG CHOLESTEROL | 475MG SODIUM

MUSHROOM-MARSALA SKILLET CHICKEN

STOVE Marsala, a fortified wine from Sicily with a rich, smoky flavor, is available either dry or sweet. Dry marsala, sometimes served as an apéritif, is used in Italian cooking to flavor a number of popular dishes such as Chicken Marsala. Sweet marsala is used as a dessert wine, as well as a flavoring for desserts such as zabaglione.

TOTAL TIME: 30 MINUTES

MAKES: 4 SERVINGS

4 MEDIUM SKINLESS, BONELESS CHICKEN BREAST HALVES (1¼ POUNDS)	1 LARGE SHALLOT, FINELY CHOPPED
⅛ TEASPOON GROUND BLACK PEPPER	½ CUP REDUCED-SODIUM CHICKEN BROTH
½ TEASPOON SALT	½ CUP DRY MARSALA WINE
1 TABLESPOON OLIVE OIL	2 TABLESPOONS CHOPPED FRESH PARSLEY
1 PACKAGE (10 OUNCES) SLICED CREMINI MUSHROOMS	

1   With meat mallet, pound chicken breast halves to even ½-inch thickness (or place chicken between two sheets of plastic wrap or waxed paper and pound with rolling pin). Sprinkle with pepper and ¼ teaspoon salt.

2   In nonstick 12-inch skillet, heat oil over medium heat until hot. Add chicken breasts and cook, turning once, until browned on both sides and chicken loses pink color throughout, 6 to 7 minutes. Transfer chicken breasts to platter; cover loosely with foil to keep warm.

3   To same skillet, add mushrooms, shallot, and remaining ¼ teaspoon salt. Cook, stirring frequently, until mushrooms are browned, 3 minutes. Add broth, wine, and any juices from platter; cook, stirring occasionally, until sauce is reduced by half, about 4 minutes. Stir in parsley. To serve, spoon sauce over chicken.

EACH SERVING: ABOUT 220 CALORIES | 36G PROTEIN | 4G CARBOHYDRATE | 5G TOTAL FAT (1G SATURATED) | 2G FIBER | 82MG CHOLESTEROL | 470MG SODIUM

GREEN-CHILE SKILLET CHICKEN

 This Tex-Mex specialty relies on canned green chiles for its heat. You can choose the ones labeled mild, medium, or hot, depending on your preference.

TOTAL TIME: 20 MINUTES

MAKES: 4 SERVINGS

4   MEDIUM SKINLESS, BONELESS CHICKEN BREAST HALVES (1¼ POUNDS)

¼   TEASPOON SALT

⅛   TEASPOON GROUND BLACK PEPPER

1   TABLESPOON OLIVE OIL

1   CAN (4 TO 4½ OUNCES) DICED GREEN CHILES, DRAINED

1   CUP GRAPE TOMATOES, EACH CUT IN HALF

¾   CUP REDUCED-SODIUM CHICKEN BROTH

½   TEASPOON GROUND CUMIN

1   GARLIC CLOVE, CRUSHED WITH GARLIC PRESS

2   TABLESPOONS CHOPPED FRESH CILANTRO

1   With meat mallet, pound chicken breast halves to even ½-inch thickness (or place chicken between two sheets of plastic wrap or waxed paper and pound with rolling pin). Sprinkle with salt and pepper.

2   In nonstick 12-inch skillet, heat oil over medium heat until hot. Add chicken breasts and cook, turning once, until browned on both sides and chicken loses its pink color throughout, 6 to 7 minutes. Transfer chicken breasts to platter; cover loosely with foil to keep warm.

3   To skillet, add chiles, tomatoes, broth, cumin, garlic, and juices from platter; cook, stirring occasionally, until sauce is slightly reduced, about 3 minutes. Stir in cilantro. To serve, spoon sauce over chicken.

EACH SERVING: ABOUT 205 CALORIES | 33G PROTEIN | 4G CARBOHYDRATE | 5G TOTAL FAT (1G SATURATED) | 0G FIBER | 82MG CHOLESTEROL | 445MG SODIUM

CHICKEN TIKKA MASALA

 STOVE **Enjoy tender chunks of chicken in a rich sauce redolent of the flavors of India. Our version puts dinner on the table in a snap.**

ACTIVE TIME: 10 MINUTES · **TOTAL TIME:** 25 MINUTES
MAKES: 4 SERVINGS

1 CUP BASMATI RICE	¼ TEASPOON SALT
1 TABLESPOON VEGETABLE OIL	¼ TEASPOON GROUND BLACK PEPPER
1 MEDIUM ONION, CHOPPED	1 CUP CRUSHED TOMATO
2 TEASPOONS GRATED PEELED FRESH GINGER	½ CUP HALF-AND-HALF OR LIGHT CREAM
1 CLOVE GARLIC, CRUSHED WITH PRESS	¼ CUP LOOSELY PACKED FRESH CILANTRO LEAVES, CHOPPED, PLUS ADDITIONAL FOR GARNISH
2 TABLESPOONS INDIAN CURRY PASTE	
1¼ POUNDS SKINLESS, BONELESS CHICKEN BREAST HALVES, CUT INTO 1-INCH CHUNKS	

1   Prepare rice as label directs.

2   Meanwhile, in nonstick 12-inch skillet, heat oil on medium 1 minute. Add onion and cook 6 minutes, stirring frequently. Add ginger, garlic, and curry paste; cook 3 minutes longer.

3   Add chicken, salt, and pepper and cook 2 minutes or until no longer pink on the outside, stirring occasionally. Add tomato; cover and cook 3 to 4 minutes longer or until chicken just loses its pink color throughout.

4   Stir in half-and-half and cilantro. Spoon rice into 4 shallow bowls; top with chicken mixture and garnish with additional chopped cilantro.

EACH SERVING: ABOUT 430 CALORIES | 39G PROTEIN | 42G CARBOHYDRATE | 13G TOTAL FAT (4G SATURATED) | 6G FIBER | 93MG CHOLESTEROL | 685MG SODIUM

LEMON-MINT CHICKEN BREASTS ON WATERCRESS

GRILL It doesn't get much fresher (or faster to prepare!) than this chicken-on-salad creation. Peppery watercress perfectly balances our perky, mint-infused dressing.

TOTAL TIME: 20 MINUTES

MAKES: 4 SERVINGS

---

4   MEDIUM SKINLESS, BONELESS CHICKEN BREAST HALVES (1¼ POUNDS)

2   LEMONS

2   TABLESPOONS OLIVE OIL

3   TABLESPOONS CHOPPED FRESH MINT (SEE TIP)

½   TEASPOON SALT

¼   TEASPOON COARSELY GROUND BLACK PEPPER

1   BAG (4 OUNCES) BABY WATERCRESS

1   Prepare grill for direct grilling over medium-high heat, or heat ridged grill pan over medium-high heat.

2   With meat mallet, pound chicken breast halves to even ¼-inch thickness (or place chicken between two sheets of plastic wrap or waxed paper and pound with rolling pin).

3   From lemons, grate 1 tablespoon plus 1½ teaspoons peel and squeeze 3 tablespoons juice. In large bowl, whisk lemon peel and juice, oil, 2 tablespoons mint, salt, and pepper until blended.

4   Reserve ¼ cup dressing. In large bowl, toss chicken breasts with remaining dressing. Place chicken on grill over medium-high heat and grill, turning once, until juices run clear when breast is pierced with tip of knife, 4 to 5 minutes.

5   Meanwhile, in large bowl, toss watercress with reserved dressing. To serve, divide watercress among dinner plates and top each with chicken. Sprinkle with remaining chopped mint.

TIP Fresh mint is often paired with lemon in Mediterranean cooking. But if mint isn't available, substitute fresh basil or flat-leaf parsley.

EACH SERVING: ABOUT 225 CALORIES | 34G PROTEIN | 2G CARBOHYDRATE | 9G TOTAL FAT (1G SATURATED) | 1G FIBER | 82MG CHOLESTEROL | 375MG SODIUM

CHICKEN WITH SMASHED POTATOES, POTPIE STYLE

 News flash, potpie lovers! There's no need to spend precious time preparing a crust when what you really want is the filling!

ACTIVE TIME: 10 MINUTES · **TOTAL TIME:** 30 MINUTES

MAKES: 4 SERVINGS

1½ POUNDS BABY RED POTATOES, EACH CUT IN HALF

1 TABLESPOON VEGETABLE OIL

4 MEDIUM SKINLESS, BONELESS CHICKEN-BREAST HALVES (ABOUT 1¼ POUNDS)

½ TEASPOON SALT

¼ TEASPOON GROUND BLACK PEPPER

2 MEDIUM CARROTS, CUT INTO 2" BY ¼" MATCHSTICK STRIPS (ABOUT 1½ CUPS)

1 CUP CHICKEN BROTH

¼ CUP HEAVY OR WHIPPING CREAM

½ TEASPOON DRIED TARRAGON, CRUMBLED

1 CUP TINY FROZEN PEAS, THAWED

1 TABLESPOON BUTTER OR MARGARINE

FRESH TARRAGON SPRIGS FOR GARNISH (OPTIONAL)

1 In 5-quart Dutch oven, combine potatoes and enough *water* to cover; heat to boiling over high heat. Reduce heat to medium; cover and simmer until potatoes are fork-tender, about 12 minutes.

2 Meanwhile, in 12-inch skillet, heat oil over medium-high heat until very hot. Add chicken and sprinkle with ¼ teaspoon salt and ⅛ teaspoon pepper; cook 6 minutes. Turn chicken over and reduce heat to medium; cover and cook until juices run clear when thickest part of chicken is pierced with knife, about 8 minutes longer. Transfer chicken to plate; keep warm.

3 To same skillet, add carrots, broth, cream, and dried tarragon; cover and cook over medium-high heat until carrots are tender, about 5 minutes. Remove skillet from heat and stir in peas.

4 Drain potatoes and return to pot. Coarsely mash potatoes with butter and remaining ¼ teaspoon salt and ⅛ teaspoon pepper.

5 To serve, spoon potatoes onto large platter; top with chicken and spoon vegetable mixture over all. Garnish with tarragon sprigs, if desired.

EACH SERVING: ABOUT 455 CALORIES | 39G PROTEIN | 43G CARBOHYDRATE | 14G TOTAL FAT (4G SATURATED) | 5G FIBER | 110MG CHOLESTEROL | 637MG SODIUM

CURRIED CHICKEN AND FRUIT SALAD

NO COOK A perfect main course for a sultry summer evening, this tasty salad is as easy on the cook as it is on the waistline. It's simpler to remove the skin and chop the meat while the bird is still warm, so prep it as soon as you get home. Then cover and refrigerate until you're ready to start dinner.

TOTAL TIME: 15 MINUTES

MAKES: 4 SERVINGS

¼ CUP MANGO CHUTNEY

¼ CUP LIGHT MAYONNAISE

2 TABLESPOONS FRESH LIME JUICE

2 TEASPOONS CURRY POWDER

10 OUNCES SKINLESS ROTISSERIE CHICKEN MEAT, CUT INTO ½-INCH PIECES (2 CUPS)

2 MEDIUM STALKS CELERY, CHOPPED

¼ RIPE MEDIUM CANTALOUPE, CUT INTO ¾-INCH PIECES (1½ CUPS)

1 CUP SEEDLESS RED GRAPES, EACH CUT IN HALF

8 BOSTON LETTUCE LEAVES

1   Coarsely chop any large pieces of fruit in chutney. In large bowl, combine chutney, mayonnaise, lime juice, and curry powder; stir until blended. Stir in chicken, celery, cantaloupe, and grapes.

2   To serve, divide lettuce among 4 dinner plates; top each with chicken salad.

EACH SERVING: ABOUT 270 CALORIES | 22G PROTEIN | 23G CARBOHYDRATE | 11G TOTAL FAT (3G SATURATED) | 3G FIBER | 68MG CHOLESTEROL | 220MG SODIUM

CHICKEN SOUP WITH LATIN FLAVORS

This is a wonderful north-of-the-border version of tortilla soup. If fresh corn is unavailable, you can substitute frozen whole-kernel corn (no need to thaw it beforehand), but you will sacrifice a bit of flavor.

ACTIVE TIME: 20 MINUTES · TOTAL TIME: 30 MINUTES

MAKES: 4 SERVINGS

1 TABLESPOON VEGETABLE OIL	2 TABLESPOONS FRESH LIME JUICE
2 GARLIC CLOVES, CHOPPED	10 OUNCES SKINLESS ROTISSERIE CHICKEN MEAT, CUT INTO ½-INCH PIECES (2 CUPS)
2 MEDIUM CARROTS, PEELED AND CHOPPED	
2 MEDIUM STALKS CELERY, CHOPPED	½ CUP LOOSELY PACKED FRESH CILANTRO LEAVES, COARSELY CHOPPED
1 MEDIUM ONION, CHOPPED	
½ JALAPEÑO CHILE WITH SEEDS, THINLY SLICED	2 PLUM TOMATOES, CUT INTO ½-INCH PIECES
1 TEASPOON GROUND CUMIN	1 RIPE MEDIUM AVOCADO, PITTED, PEELED, AND CUT INTO ½-INCH PIECES
4 CUPS CHICKEN BROTH	
1½ CUPS WATER	LIME WEDGES
1 CUP CORN KERNELS CUT FROM COBS (2 EARS)	TORTILLA CHIPS (OPTIONAL)

1 In 6-quart saucepot, heat oil over low heat until hot. Add garlic, carrots, celery, onion, and jalapeño. Cover and cook, stirring frequently, until vegetables are tender, 8 to 10 minutes. Add cumin and cook, stirring, 30 seconds. Add broth and water; cover and heat to boiling over high heat.
2 Stir corn, lime juice, chicken pieces, and cilantro into broth mixture; heat to boiling over high heat. Remove from heat; stir in tomato pieces.
3 Ladle soup into 4 warm large soup bowls; sprinkle with avocado pieces. Serve with lime wedges and, if you like, tortilla chips.

EACH SERVING: ABOUT 365 CALORIES | 27G PROTEIN | 26G CARBOHYDRATE | 19G TOTAL FAT (3G SATURATED) | 6G FIBER | 63MG CHOLESTEROL | 1,205MG SODIUM

DOUBLE-DIPPED POTATO-CHIP CHICKEN WITH QUICK SLAW

OVEN The potato-chip coating on this chicken and the cabbage-and-carrot slaw earn this dish an A+ for crunch and texture. You can also substitute the preshredded broccoli "slaw" that's usually found in your supermarket's refrigerated produce case. For photo, see page 18.

ACTIVE TIME: 20 MINUTES · **TOTAL TIME:** 30 MINUTES
MAKES: 4 SERVINGS

1¼ CUPS CRUSHED POTATO CHIPS

1 LARGE EGG

4 MEDIUM SKINLESS, BONELESS CHICKEN BREAST HALVES (1¼ POUNDS)

⅜ TEASPOON GROUND BLACK PEPPER

4 CUPS PRESHREDDED CABBAGE MIX FOR COLESLAW

1 LARGE CARROT, PEELED AND SHREDDED

¼ SMALL RED ONION, THINLY SLICED

¼ CUP CIDER VINEGAR

1 TABLESPOON VEGETABLE OIL

1 TEASPOON SUGAR

½ TEASPOON SALT

¼ CUP LIGHT MAYONNAISE

2 TABLESPOONS BARBECUE SAUCE

1 Preheat oven to 450°F.

2 Place crushed chips on large plate. With fork, beat egg in pie plate or shallow dish. Dip 1 piece chicken in egg, then coat with crumbs, pressing chicken so crumbs adhere. Transfer chicken to ungreased cookie sheet. Repeat with remaining chicken.

3 Dip each piece chicken again in remaining crumbs to coat completely. Return chicken to cookie sheet. Sprinkle both sides of chicken with ¼ teaspoon pepper. Bake just until chicken loses its pink color throughout, about 15 minutes.

4 Meanwhile, in large bowl, toss cabbage mix with carrot, onion, vinegar, oil, sugar, salt, and remaining ⅛ teaspoon pepper until well combined. In small bowl, stir mayonnaise and barbecue sauce until well blended.

5 To serve, spoon barbecue mayonnaise into 4 small cups. Divide chicken and slaw among 4 dinner plates and serve with mayonnaise.

EACH SERVING: ABOUT 460 CALORIES | 38G PROTEIN | 30G CARBOHYDRATE | 21G TOTAL FAT (4G SATURATED) | 5G FIBER | 140MG CHOLESTEROL | 755MG SODIUM

5 IDEAS FOR...BAGGED SLAW

Prepackaged bagged slaw (16 ounces) adds vitamins—and lots of crunch!—to these quick entrées and side dishes.

Moo Shu Chicken: In large nonstick skillet, cook 1 package shredded cabbage, ⅓ cup bottled stir-fry sauce, and 4 sliced green onions over medium heat about 4 minutes, stirring often. Stir in 2 cups shredded cooked chicken (10 ounces); heat through. Warm 4 (8-inch) flour tortillas and fill with Moo Shu mixture. Makes 4 main-dish servings.

Wilted Cabbage and Bacon: Chop 3 slices fully cooked bacon and thinly slice 1 small red onion; place in a large nonstick skillet and cook over medium heat about 4 minutes, stirring occasionally. Stir in 1 package shredded cabbage, 1 cup shredded carrots, 3 tablespoons cider vinegar, and ½ teaspoon salt; cook until tender-crisp. Makes 6 side-dish servings.

Waldorf Slaw: In large bowl, toss 1 package shredded cabbage with 1 cored and chopped Red Delicious apple, 2 stalks chopped celery, ½ cup chopped walnuts, ⅔ cup bottled poppy-seed salad dressing, and ½ teaspoon salt. Makes 8 side-dish servings.

Caribbean Pineapple Coleslaw: Drain 1 can (20 ounces) pineapple chunks in juice; place in large bowl. Add 1 package shredded cabbage, 2 tablespoons packed brown sugar, 2 tablespoons olive oil, 2 teaspoons grated fresh lime peel, 5 tablespoons fresh lime juice, and ½ teaspoon salt. Toss until well mixed. Makes 6 side-dish servings.

Smoky Tomato and Cabbage Soup: In large microwave-safe bowl, combine ½ package shredded cabbage (4 cups), ¾ cup chopped sweet onion, and 1 tablespoon olive oil. Cover and microwave on High about 4 minutes or until vegetables soften, stirring halfway through. In blender, with center part of cover removed to let steam escape, puree cabbage mixture, 1 can (28 ounces) fire-roasted diced tomatoes, 1 cup water, and 2 teaspoons red wine vinegar. Serve at room temperature or heat in microwave on High 3 minutes to serve hot. Makes 6 first-course servings.

BUFFALO CHICKEN BURGERS

GRILL Fans of Buffalo chicken wings will love these savory burgers, which are grilled and then served with the traditional fixin's: blue cheese sauce and carrot and celery sticks.

ACTIVE TIME: 20 MINUTES · **TOTAL TIME:** 30 MINUTES

MAKES: 4 SERVINGS

¼ CUP LIGHT MAYONNAISE

¼ CUP REDUCED-FAT SOUR CREAM

2 OUNCES BLUE CHEESE, CRUMBLED (½ CUP)

2 TEASPOONS CIDER VINEGAR

½ TEASPOON WORCESTERSHIRE SAUCE

1¼ POUNDS GROUND CHICKEN OR TURKEY

1 LARGE STALK CELERY, FINELY CHOPPED, PLUS ADDITIONAL STALKS CUT INTO STICKS FOR SERVING

3 TABLESPOONS CAYENNE PEPPER SAUCE, PLUS ADDITIONAL FOR SERVING

NONSTICK COOKING SPRAY

4 HAMBURGER BUNS, SPLIT AND TOASTED

LETTUCE LEAVES

CARROT STICKS

1 Preheat grill pan or prepare grill for direct grilling over medium heat.

2 In small bowl, stir mayonnaise, sour cream, blue cheese, vinegar, and Worcestershire until blended; set aside. Makes about ¾ cup.

3 In medium bowl, with hands, combine chicken, celery, and cayenne pepper sauce just until blended but not overmixed. Shape mixture into four ¾-inch-thick burgers. Spray both sides of burgers with nonstick cooking spray.

4 Place burgers on grill over medium heat; grill, turning once, until meat loses its pink color throughout, 12 to 14 minutes. Burgers should reach an internal temperature of 165°F.

5 Serve burgers on buns with lettuce and some blue cheese sauce. Serve remaining sauce with carrot and celery sticks. Pass additional cayenne pepper sauce, if you like.

EACH BURGER WITH BUN: ABOUT 345 CALORIES | 27G PROTEIN | 22G CARBOHYDRATE 16G TOTAL FAT (1G SATURATED) | 1G FIBER | 0MG CHOLESTEROL | 785MG SODIUM

EACH TABLESPOON BLUE CHEESE SAUCE: ABOUT 40 CALORIES | 1G PROTEIN | 1G CARBOHYDRATE | 4G TOTAL FAT (2G SATURATED) | 0G FIBER | 7MG CHOLESTEROL | 110MG SODIUM

TURKEY PITA-POCKET BURGERS

 GRILL **Pita pockets, yogurt, feta, and mint add a taste of Greece to this flavorful (but slimmed-down) summer favorite.**

TOTAL TIME: 25 MINUTES

MAKES: 4 SERVINGS

½ CUP PLUS 2 TABLESPOONS PLAIN FAT-FREE YOGURT

2 GREEN ONIONS, GREEN AND WHITE PARTS SEPARATED AND THINLY SLICED

½ CUP PACKED FRESH MINT LEAVES, FINELY CHOPPED

1 POUND LEAN GROUND TURKEY

1½ OUNCES FETA CHEESE (ABOUT ⅓ CUP), FINELY CRUMBLED

1½ TEASPOONS GROUND CORIANDER

⅛ TEASPOON SALT

⅛ TEASPOON GROUND BLACK PEPPER

2 WHOLE-WHEAT PITAS, CUT IN HALF

2 TOMATOES, THINLY SLICED

1   Prepare outdoor grill for covered direct grilling over medium heat.

2   In small bowl, combine ½ cup yogurt, white parts of green onions, and ¼ cup chopped mint.

3   In large bowl, with hands, combine turkey, feta, coriander, salt, pepper, green parts of green onions, remaining ¼ cup mint, and remaining 2 tablespoons yogurt. Mix well, then form into patties 3½-inches round and ¾-inch thick.

4   Place turkey patties on hot grill grate; cover and cook 12 to 13 minutes or just until meat loses its pink color throughout, turning once. (Burgers should reach an internal temperature of 165°F.) During last 2 minutes of cooking, add pitas to grill. Heat 2 minutes or until warmed, turning once.

5   Open pitas. Divide burgers, tomato slices, and yogurt sauce among pitas.

EACH SERVING: ABOUT 310 CALORIES | 30G PROTEIN | 24G CARBOHYDRATE | 12G TOTAL FAT (4G SATURATED FAT) | 4G FIBER | 90MG CHOLESTEROL | 460MG SODIUM

TURKEY CUTLETS WITH PEARS AND TARRAGON

 This good-for-you recipe contains lean proteins (turkey) and green veggies (spinach). The best pears for this recipe are Anjou and Bosc, which are juicy and keep their shape when cooked.

TOTAL TIME: 25 MINUTES

MAKES: 4 SERVINGS

1 TABLESPOON OLIVE OIL	1 CUP CHICKEN BROTH
4 TURKEY BREAST CUTLETS (ABOUT 1 POUND)	¼ CUP DRIED TART CHERRIES OR CRANBERRIES
¼ TEASPOON SALT	2 TABLESPOONS DIJON MUSTARD WITH SEEDS
⅛ TEASPOON GROUND BLACK PEPPER	
2 LARGE FIRM, RIPE PEARS, PEELED, CORED, AND CUT INTO ½-INCH-THICK WEDGES (SEE TIP)	½ TEASPOON DRIED TARRAGON
	1 BAG (9 OUNCES) MICROWAVE-IN-THE-BAG SPINACH

1 In 12-inch skillet, heat oil over high heat until hot. Sprinkle turkey breast cutlets with salt and pepper. Add cutlets to skillet and cook, turning once, until turkey is golden brown on both sides and has just lost pink color throughout, 3 to 4 minutes. Transfer cutlets to plate; keep warm.

2 To same skillet, add pears. Reduce heat to medium-high and cook pears, turning occasionally, until browned, about 3 minutes. Add broth, cherries, Dijon mustard, and tarragon to skillet. Increase heat to high and cook, stirring occasionally, until sauce thickens slightly and pears are tender, 4 to 5 minutes.

3 Meanwhile, in microwave oven, cook spinach in bag as label directs.

4 Return cutlets to skillet; heat through, spooning pear sauce over cutlets.

5 To serve, spoon spinach onto 4 dinner plates. Top with turkey, pears, and sauce.

TIP Peel and cut the pears just before you are ready to use them; like cut apples, they discolor. If you want to prep them in advance, place them in a bowl of cold water to which you've added 1 teaspoon lemon juice. Drain and pat dry before using.

EACH SERVING: ABOUT 255 CALORIES | 31G PROTEIN | 20G CARBOHYDRATE | 6G TOTAL FAT (1G SATURATED) | 8G FIBER | 71MG CHOLESTEROL | 565MG SODIUM

TURKEY AND WHITE BEAN CHILI

 This cumin-scented turkey chili is healthy and ready in a hurry! Serve with store-bought or homemade cornbread.

STOVE

ACTIVE TIME: 15 MINUTES · **TOTAL TIME:** 20 MINUTES

MAKES: 4 SERVINGS

1 TABLESPOON OLIVE OIL	1 CAN (4 TO 4½ OUNCES) CHOPPED MILD GREEN CHILES, NOT DRAINED
1 MEDIUM ONION, CHOPPED	
1 POUND LEAN GROUND TURKEY	1 CAN (14½ OUNCES) CHICKEN BROTH
2 TEASPOONS GROUND CORIANDER	2 SMALL RIPE TOMATOES (ABOUT 4 OUNCES EACH), COARSELY CHOPPED
2 TEASPOONS GROUND CUMIN	
2 TEASPOONS FRESH THYME LEAVES	1 LIME, CUT INTO WEDGES
2 CANS (15 TO 19 OUNCES EACH) GREAT NORTHERN BEANS, RINSED AND DRAINED	

1 In 12-inch skillet, heat oil over medium-high heat. Add onion and cook, stirring frequently, until tender and golden, about 5 minutes. Add turkey and cook, breaking up turkey with side of spoon, until it loses its pink color throughout, about 5 minutes. Stir in coriander, cumin, and thyme; cook, stirring frequently, 1 minute.

2 Meanwhile, in small bowl, mash half of beans.

3 Stir mashed beans, remaining whole beans, chiles with their liquid, and broth into turkey mixture; heat to boiling over medium-high heat. Boil until chili has thickened slightly, about 1 minute. Stir in tomatoes. Serve with lime wedges.

EACH SERVING: ABOUT 495 CALORIES | 35G PROTEIN | 49G CARBOHYDRATE | 18G TOTAL FAT (4G SATURATED) | 10G FIBER | 90MG CHOLESTEROL | 1,040MG SODIUM

TURKEY ENCHILADAS

OVEN

These zesty enchiladas feature roasted turkey breast from the deli counter and canned enchilada sauce, so you can get a satisfying family meal on the table in a jiffy.

ACTIVE TIME: 10 MINUTES · TOTAL TIME: 30 MINUTES
MAKES: 5 SERVINGS

12 OUNCES ROASTED BONELESS TURKEY BREAST (FROM THE DELI), CHOPPED

1 CAN (8¾ OUNCES) NO-SALT-ADDED CORN, DRAINED

1 CONTAINER (8 OUNCES) REDUCED-FAT SOUR CREAM

1½ CUPS SHREDDED REDUCED-FAT (2%) MEXICAN CHEESE BLEND

2 TABLESPOONS CHOPPED FRESH CILANTRO

10 (6-INCH) CORN TORTILLAS, WARMED TO SOFTEN

1 CAN (10 OUNCES) ENCHILADA SAUCE

1 CUP MILD SALSA

1 Preheat oven to 400°F. Spray 13" by 19" baking dish with nonstick cooking spray.

2 In large bowl, combine turkey, corn, sour cream, ¾ cup cheese, and 1 tablespoon cilantro.

3 Place about ⅓ cup turkey mixture on each tortilla and roll up tightly. Arrange in prepared baking dish, seam side down. Repeat with remaining tortillas and filling.

4 In bowl, stir enchilada sauce with salsa; pour over tortillas to cover. Top with remaining ¾ cup cheese and bake 15 to 20 minutes or until cheese melts and enchiladas are heated through. Sprinkle with remaining 1 tablespoon cilantro.

EACH SERVING: ABOUT 445 CALORIES | 34G PROTEIN | 42G CARBOHYDRATE | 16G TOTAL FAT (7G SATURATED FAT) | 6G FIBER | 98MG CHOLESTEROL | 725MG SODIUM

CRISPY DUCK BREASTS WITH CHERRY SAUCE

STOVE This streamlined classic recipe is also great made with pork. You can substitute two 6-ounce, ¾-inch-thick) boneless pork loin chops for the duck. In step 2, season the chops and cook them in 1 teaspoon vegetable oil over medium heat, for about 8 minutes, turning them once. Then proceed as directed.

ACTIVE TIME: 25 MINUTES · TOTAL TIME: 30 MINUTES

MAKES: 4 SERVINGS

1   PACKAGE (6 OUNCES) WHITE-AND-WILD RICE BLEND, COOKED (OPTIONAL)

4   SMALL DUCK BREAST HALVES (6 OUNCES EACH)

½   TEASPOON SALT

½   TEASPOON GROUND BLACK PEPPER

⅔   CUP PORT WINE

2   CANS (14½ OUNCES) TART CHERRIES IN WATER, WELL DRAINED

¼   CUP SUGAR

STEAMED GREEN BEANS (OPTIONAL)

1   Prepare rice as label directs. Keep warm.

2   Meanwhile, pat duck breasts dry with paper towels. Make several ¼-inch-deep diagonal slashes in duck skin. Place breasts, skin side down, in nonstick 10-inch skillet; sprinkle with salt and pepper. Cook over medium heat until skin is deep brown, about 12 minutes; turn breasts and cook 3 minutes longer for medium. Transfer breasts, skin side down, to cutting board; let stand 5 minutes for easier slicing. Discard fat from skillet but do not wash.

3   While duck is standing, add port to skillet; heat to boiling over medium heat. Boil until reduced by half, about 5 minutes. Add cherries and sugar and simmer, stirring occasionally, until most of liquid has evaporated, 3 to 4 minutes.

4   To serve, slice breasts crosswise. Transfer slices, skin side up, to 4 dinner plates. Spoon cherry sauce over duck. Serve with rice and green beans, if you like.

EACH SERVING: ABOUT 320 CALORIES | 23G PROTEIN | 36G CARBOHYDRATE | 10G TOTAL FAT (3G SATURATED) | 1G FIBER | 120MG CHOLESTEROL | 380MG SODIUM

BEEF, PORK & LAMB

BLT Burgers (page 67)

SKIRT STEAK WITH CHIMICHURRI SAUCE

GRILL In Argentina, where grilled meat is a staple, chimichurri is the accompaniment of choice. This tasty green sauce, similar in texture to pesto, is also great drizzled over chicken or veggies and makes an excellent sandwich spread. If you have any left over, refrigerate it in a container with a tight-fitting lid for up to two days. Bring it to room temperature before serving.

ACTIVE TIME: 15 MINUTES · **TOTAL TIME:** 30 MINUTES
MAKES: 4 SERVINGS

CHIMICHURRI SAUCE

- 1 GARLIC CLOVE, CRUSHED WITH GARLIC PRESS
- ¼ TEASPOON SALT
- 1 CUP LOOSELY PACKED FRESH FLAT-LEAF PARSLEY LEAVES, CHOPPED
- 1 CUP LOOSELY PACKED FRESH CILANTRO LEAVES, CHOPPED
- 2 TABLESPOONS OLIVE OIL
- 1 TABLESPOON RED WINE VINEGAR
- ¼ TEASPOON CRUSHED RED PEPPER

STEAK

- 1 BEEF SKIRT STEAK OR FLANK STEAK (1¼ POUNDS)
- ¼ TEASPOON SALT
- ⅛ TEASPOON COARSELY GROUND BLACK PEPPER

1 Prepare sauce: In small bowl, with fork, stir garlic, salt, parsley, cilantro, oil, vinegar, and crushed red pepper until mixed. (Or, in mini food processor or blender, puree sauce ingredients until smooth.) Makes about ¼ cup.

2 Prepare grill for covered direct grilling over medium heat.

3 Sprinkle steak with salt and pepper. Place on grill over medium heat; cover and grill steak 3 minutes per side for medium-rare or until desired doneness.

4 Transfer steak to cutting board; let stand 10 minutes to set juices for easier slicing. Thinly slice steak crosswise (against grain). Serve with chimichurri sauce.

EACH SERVING STEAK WITH 1 TABLESPOON SAUCE: ABOUT 300 CALORIES | 40G PROTEIN 1G CARBOHYDRATE | 14G TOTAL FAT (5G SATURATED) | 0G FIBER | 121MG CHOLESTEROL 380MG SODIUM

CHIPOTLE STEAK SANDWICHES

 STOVE Spread a luscious steak sandwich with chipotle-spiced mayonnaise. Complete the meal with a fresh gingery cucumber salad on the side.

ACTIVE TIME: 20 MINUTES · **TOTAL TIME:** 30 MINUTES

MAKES: 4 SERVINGS

¼ CUP LIGHT MAYONNAISE

¼ TEASPOON CHIPOTLE CHILE POWDER

1 POUND BEEF SHOULDER TOP BLADE STEAK (FLATIRON), 1 INCH THICK

¼ TEASPOON GROUND BLACK PEPPER

⅜ TEASPOON SALT

1 MEDIUM SWEET ONION, THINLY SLICED

1 TABLESPOON WATER

1 LARGE ENGLISH CUCUMBER (1 POUND), PEELED AND THINLY SLICED

1 TABLESPOON FRESH LEMON JUICE

½ TEASPOON GRATED PEELED FRESH GINGER

2 CIABATTA ROLLS, HALVED AND TOASTED

1 In small bowl, combine mayonnaise and chile powder. Set aside.

2 Heat 10-inch cast iron or other heavy skillet on medium-high heat until very hot. Season steak with pepper and ⅛ teaspoon salt; cook 15 minutes for medium or until desired doneness, turning once. Transfer to cutting board; let stand.

3 To same skillet, add onion and ⅛ teaspoon salt. Reduce heat to medium-low; cook 5 to 7 minutes or until tender, stirring.

4 Meanwhile, in medium bowl, toss cucumber, lemon juice, ginger, and remaining ⅛ teaspoon salt until well mixed.

5 Slice steak across grain. Spread chile mayonnaise on rolls; top with steak and onion. Serve sandwiches open faced with cucumber salad.

EACH SERVING: ABOUT 315 CALORIES | 25G PROTEIN | 24G CARBOHYDRATE | 14G TOTAL FAT (4G SATURATED) | 2G FIBER | 65MG CHOLESTEROL | 615MG SODIUM

CORIANDER STEAK WITH WARM CORN SALAD

 These steaks are spiced with the warm flavor of coriander and the punch of black pepper. The corn salad comes together in less than fifteen minutes.

TOTAL TIME: 25 MINUTES

MAKES: 4 SERVINGS

2 TEASPOONS OLIVE OIL	½ SMALL RED ONION, FINELY CHOPPED
1 TABLESPOON CORIANDER SEEDS, CRUSHED	2 CUPS CORN KERNELS CUT FROM COBS (ABOUT 4 EARS)
1 TEASPOON CRACKED BLACK PEPPER	1 TABLESPOON CHOPPED FRESH CILANTRO LEAVES
¾ TEASPOON SALT	1 TABLESPOON FRESH LIME JUICE
2 (10-OUNCE) BONELESS BEEF TOP LOIN STEAKS, ¾ INCH THICK	½ TEASPOON GROUND CUMIN
1 SMALL RED PEPPER, CUT INTO ¼-INCH PIECES	

1 Heat 10-inch grill pan or cast-iron skillet over medium-high heat until very hot. Brush pan with 1 teaspoon oil. On waxed paper, mix coriander, black pepper, and ½ teaspoon salt; use to coat both sides of steaks.

2 Place steaks in pan; cook, turning once, about 8 minutes for medium-rare, or until desired doneness.

3 Meanwhile, in 2-quart saucepan, heat remaining 1 teaspoon oil over medium-high heat. Add red pepper and onion; cook, stirring occasionally, until soft, about 5 minutes. Stir in corn; heat through. Stir in cilantro, lime juice, cumin, and remaining ¼ teaspoon salt. Makes about 2½ cups.

4 Transfer steak to cutting board. Let stand 5 minutes to set juices for easier slicing. Thinly slice steak and serve with corn salad.

EACH SERVING: ABOUT 430 CALORIES | 31G PROTEIN | 25G CARBOHYDRATE | 25G TOTAL FAT (9G SATURATED) | 0G FIBER | 84MG CHOLESTEROL | 705MG SODIUM

STEAK AU POIVRE

 This French classic couldn't be easier to prepare. First, you'll cook the steaks to the desired doneness in a mixture of butter and olive oil. Then, after transferring them to a warm platter, you'll whip up the luscious sauce in moments, right in the same pan. If you can't find chives, substitute finely chopped green onions.

ACTIVE TIME: 20 MINUTES · **TOTAL TIME:** 25 MINUTES

MAKES: 4 SERVINGS

1 TABLESPOON WHOLE BLACK PEPPERCORNS, CRUSHED

½ TEASPOON SALT

4 BEEF TENDERLOIN STEAKS (FILET MIGNON), 1¼ INCHES THICK (5 OUNCES EACH)

1 TABLESPOON BUTTER OR MARGARINE

1 TABLESPOON OLIVE OIL

¼ CUP DRY WHITE WINE

2 TABLESPOONS BRANDY

½ CUP HEAVY OR WHIPPING CREAM

1 TABLESPOON CHOPPED FRESH CHIVES

1 In cup, with fork, mix peppercorns and salt; use to rub on both sides of steaks.

2 In nonstick 12-inch skillet, melt butter with oil over medium heat. Add steaks and cook 7 to 8 minutes per side for medium-rare or until desired doneness. Transfer steaks to dinner plates; keep warm.

3 Add wine and brandy to skillet; heat to boiling, stirring, until browned bits are loosened from bottom of skillet. Add cream and boil until sauce has thickened, about 1 minute. Stir in chives. Pour sauce over steaks.

EACH SERVING: ABOUT 579 CALORIES | 26G PROTEIN | 2G CARBOHYDRATE | 50G TOTAL FAT (22G SATURATED) | 0G FIBER | 149MG CHOLESTEROL | 399MG SODIUM

FLANK STEAK WITH RED WINE AND OVEN FRIES

   Call it French lite: Lean flank steak has all the protein of the high-fat cuts typically used for a bistro-style "steak frites" dinner and it's also rich in iron. A side of spinach boosts the vitamin and mineral content.

ACTIVE TIME: 15 MINUTES · **TOTAL TIME:** 30 MINUTES

MAKES: 4 SERVINGS

3 MEDIUM RUSSET (BAKING) POTATOES (8 OUNCES EACH), NOT PEELED

3 TEASPOONS OLIVE OIL

½ TEASPOON SALT

¼ TEASPOON COARSELY GROUND BLACK PEPPER

1¼ POUNDS BEEF FLANK STEAK, TRIMMED OF FAT

½ TEASPOON DRIED TARRAGON

1 MEDIUM SHALLOT, MINCED

¾ CUP DRY RED WINE

1 BAG (9 OUNCES) MICROWAVE-IN-THE-BAG BABY SPINACH

1 Preheat oven to 450°F. Cut each potato crosswise in half, then cut each half lengthwise into 8 wedges.

2 Spray 15½" by 10½" jelly-roll pan with nonstick cooking spray. Place potatoes in pan and toss with 2 teaspoons oil, ¼ teaspoon salt, and pepper. Roast potatoes 25 minutes or until fork-tender and beginning to brown, stirring once halfway through roasting.

3 Meanwhile, rub steak with tarragon and remaining ¼ teaspoon salt to season both sides. Heat 12-inch cast-iron or other heavy skillet on medium-high. Add remaining 1 teaspoon oil and steak; cook 12 minutes for medium or until desired doneness, turning once. Transfer steak to cutting board. To same skillet, add shallot and cook 1 minute, stirring. Add wine and heat to boiling; boil 2 minutes or until reduced to ⅓ cup.

4 Cook spinach in microwave as label directs. Thinly slice steak and serve with wine sauce, potatoes, and spinach.

EACH SERVING: ABOUT 415 CALORIES | 35G PROTEIN | 37G CARBOHYDRATE | 14G TOTAL FAT (5G SATURATED) | 9G FIBER | 55MG CHOLESTEROL | 460MG SODIUM

5 IDEAS FOR...FLANK STEAK

Start with sliced, cooked flank steak: broil, bake, or sauté it with a dab of olive oil until done, then portion and refrigerate or freeze it to use at your convenience. With that ready and waiting, you can whip up these satisfying meals in less than ten minutes.

Greek Flank Steak Salad: Mix 1½ pounds cubed, cooked flank steak with 8 cups mixed greens, 2 cups each halved cherry tomatoes and chopped cucumber, 1 cup crumbled feta cheese, ½ cup olives, 1 tablespoon each red wine vinegar and olive oil, and salt and pepper to taste. Makes 4 servings.

Flank Steak Fajita Wraps: Heat four 8-inch whole-wheat tortillas in the microwave for 15 seconds, or until soft. Divide the following toppings among the tortillas: 12 ounces sliced, cooked flank steak; 1 cup each prepared salsa and sliced avocado; and ½ cup shredded reduced-fat cheddar cheese. Wrap the tortillas around the fillings. Heat fajitas in a large nonstick skillet, toaster oven, or microwave, or serve cold. Makes 4 wraps.

Steak Pesto Pasta: Cook 8 ounces whole-grain penne pasta according to package directions. Drain and mix with 12 ounces cubed, cooked flank steak; ½ cup prepared pesto sauce; and 4 cups each baby spinach leaves and chopped tomatoes. Makes 4 servings.

Flank Steak Fried Rice: In large skillet, heat 1 tablespoon peanut oil over medium-high heat and add 1 tablespoon each minced garlic and minced ginger, and 3 tablespoons chopped green onions; cook for 2 minutes. Add 4 cups cooked brown rice and stir, cooking 2 to 3 minutes. Add 12 ounces cubed, cooked flank steak and stir in ¼ cup soy sauce. Makes 4 servings.

Thai Steak Noodles: Prepare 8 ounces rice noodles according to package directions. Mix with 12 ounces cubed, cooked flank steak; 1 tablespoon rice vinegar; 1 tablespoon plus 2 teaspoons peanut oil; 1 tablespoon soy sauce; and 1 tablespoon each honey and chili garlic sauce (or to taste). Top with 8 sliced green onions and ¼ cup roasted peanuts. Makes 4 servings.

STIR-FRIED STEAK AND VEGETABLES

STOVE This healthy-in-a-hurry recipe contains whole grains (brown rice), yellow-orange veggies (red pepper and carrots), lean, protein-rich beef (top round steak), and green veggies (broccoli and snow peas).

TOTAL TIME: 25 MINUTES

MAKES: 4 SERVINGS

---

1   BEEF TOP ROUND STEAK (1 POUND)

⅓   CUP REDUCED-SODIUM SOY SAUCE

2   LARGE GARLIC CLOVES, CRUSHED WITH GARLIC PRESS

1   MEDIUM ONION

1   RED PEPPER

2   TEASPOONS VEGETABLE OIL

1   PACKAGE (8 OUNCES) SLICED CREMINI MUSHROOMS

2   CUPS BROCCOLI FLORETS

2   CARROTS, THINLY SLICED

3   OUNCES SNOW PEAS, TRIMMED AND CUT IN THIRDS

2   TABLESPOONS GRATED, PEELED FRESH GINGER

¾   CUP WATER

1   POUCH (8½ OUNCES) PRECOOKED BROWN RICE, HEATED AS LABEL DIRECTS

1 With knife held in slanting position, almost parallel to cutting surface, cut steak crosswise into ⅛-inch-thick slices. In medium bowl, toss steak slices with 1 tablespoon soy sauce and 1 crushed garlic clove. Let stand 5 minutes.

2 Meanwhile, cut onion in half, then cut crosswise into thin slices. Cut red pepper into ¼-inch-thick slices. Set aside.

3 In deep nonstick 12-inch skillet, heat 1 teaspoon oil over medium heat until very hot but not smoking. Add half of beef and stir frequently (stir-fry) just until beef is no longer pink, 30 to 45 seconds. Transfer beef to plate. Repeat with remaining beef, without adding more oil.

4 In same skillet, heat remaining 1 teaspoon oil until hot. Add mushrooms and onion; cover and cook, stirring occasionally, until mushrooms are browned, 3 to 4 minutes.

5 Add broccoli, carrots, snow peas, red pepper, ginger, water, and remaining soy sauce and garlic to skillet. Stir-fry until vegetables are tender-crisp, 5 to 6 minutes. Remove skillet from heat; stir in beef with its juices. Serve over rice.

EACH SERVING: ABOUT 380 CALORIES | 34G PROTEIN | 34G CARBOHYDRATE | 12G TOTAL FAT (4G SATURATED) | 7G FIBER | 68MG CHOLESTEROL | 790MG SODIUM

MONGOLIAN BEEF STIR-FRY

STOVE This mouth-watering stir-fry gets its sweet-hot flavor from bottled hoisin sauce, a Chinese staple that you'll find in the Asian food section of most supermarkets and in Asian markets. A mixture of soybeans, garlic, chile peppers, and spices, it is used to flavor innumerable dishes. Tightly closed, hoisin will keep indefinitely in the refrigerator.

TOTAL TIME: 30 MINUTES

MAKES: 4 SERVINGS

1	BEEF FLANK STEAK (1 POUND), THINLY SLICED	1	MEDIUM RED PEPPER, THINLY SLICED
1	TABLESPOON CORNSTARCH	2	BUNCHES GREEN ONIONS, CUT INTO 3-INCH PIECES
1	TABLESPOON GRATED, PEELED FRESH GINGER	2	GARLIC CLOVES, THINLY SLICED
4	TABLESPOONS SOY SAUCE	2	TABLESPOONS DRY SHERRY
2	TABLESPOONS VEGETABLE OIL	2	TABLESPOONS HOISIN SAUCE
1	MEDIUM ONION, THINLY SLICED	1	TEASPOON SUGAR
		⅛	TEASPOON CRUSHED RED PEPPER

1 In large bowl, toss steak with cornstarch, ginger, and 2 tablespoons soy sauce until evenly coated; set aside.

2 In nonstick 12-inch skillet, heat 1 tablespoon oil over medium heat until very hot. Add onion, red pepper, green onions, and garlic; cook, stirring frequently (stir-frying), until vegetables are tender-crisp, 5 minutes.

3 Meanwhile, in cup, with fork, mix sherry, hoisin, sugar, crushed red pepper, and remaining 2 tablespoons soy sauce until blended.

4 Transfer vegetables to bowl. In same skillet, heat remaining 1 tablespoon oil over medium heat. Add beef mixture; stir-fry until lightly browned, about 2 minutes. Stir in sherry mixture; heat to boiling. Return vegetables to skillet; heat through.

EACH SERVING: ABOUT 360 CALORIES | 26G PROTEIN | 20G CARBOHYDRATE | 19G TOTAL FAT (6G SATURATED) | 4G FIBER | 59MG CHOLESTEROL | 1,205MG SODIUM

SPICY BEEF WITH COUSCOUS

 STOVE This curry is on the milder side, so it's great for the whole family. If you prefer it hotter, you can add a drop or two of hot pepper sauce. The addition of raisins to the couscous lends an unexpected sweetness.

TOTAL TIME: 30 MINUTES

MAKES: 4 SERVINGS

1 TABLESPOON VEGETABLE OIL	1 SMALL YELLOW SUMMER SQUASH (6 OUNCES), CUT INTO ½-INCH PIECES
1 MEDIUM ONION, CHOPPED	1 CUP CHICKEN BROTH
1 GARLIC CLOVE, CRUSHED WITH GARLIC PRESS	1 CUP FROZEN PEAS
1 TEASPOON MINCED, PEELED FRESH GINGER	½ CUP LOOSELY PACKED FRESH CILANTRO LEAVES, CHOPPED
1 POUND LEAN (90%) GROUND BEEF	1 CUP PLAIN COUSCOUS (MOROCCAN PASTA)
1 TABLESPOON CURRY POWDER	⅓ CUP GOLDEN RAISINS
1 TEASPOON GARAM MASALA (SEE TIP)	
½ TEASPOON SALT	

1 In nonstick 12-inch skillet, heat oil over medium heat. Add onion and cook, stirring, until golden, about 3 minutes. Stir in garlic and ginger; cook 1 minute.

2 Stir in ground beef and cook, breaking up meat with side of spoon, until meat is no longer pink, about 5 minutes. Stir in curry powder, garam masala, and salt; cook 30 seconds. Add squash and cook 2 minutes. Add broth and frozen peas; cook until thickened slightly. Stir in cilantro.

3 Meanwhile, prepare couscous as label directs but add raisins to water.

4 Fluff couscous with fork and serve with beef mixture.

TIP Garam masala is a blend of dry-roasted, ground spices that can include black pepper, cinnamon, cloves, coriander, cumin, cardamom, and dried chiles. Look for garam masala in Indian markets and in the spice section of some supermarkets.

EACH SERVING: ABOUT 520 CALORIES | 34G PROTEIN | 57G CARBOHYDRATE | 16G TOTAL FAT (5G SATURATED) | 7G FIBER | 69MG CHOLESTEROL | 650MG SODIUM

SWEET AND TANGY BRAISED CHUCK ROAST

SLOW Gingersnap cookies and raisins balance vinegar to give a sweet-and-sour flavor to the classic chuck roast. Using a slow cooker makes this tough cut tender and yields a rich, delicious sauce.

ACTIVE TIME: 10 MINUTES · **SLOW COOK:** ABOUT 8 HOURS ON LOW OR 6 HOURS ON HIGH
MAKES: 6 SERVINGS

6   (2-INCH) GINGERSNAP COOKIES, FINELY CRUSHED INTO CRUMBS

2   CUPS (ABOUT HALF 16-OUNCE BAG) PEELED BABY CARROTS

2   LARGE STALKS CELERY, CUT CROSSWISE INTO 2-INCH PIECES

1   MEDIUM ONION, CUT INTO 1-INCH PIECES

1   CUP DRY RED WINE

2   TABLESPOONS RED WINE VINEGAR

¼   CUP RAISINS

1   TEASPOON SALT

½   TEASPOON GROUND BLACK PEPPER

1   BONELESS BEEF CHUCK ROAST (ABOUT 2 POUNDS)

1   In 4½- to 6-quart slow-cooker pot, combine gingersnap crumbs, carrots, celery, onion, wine, vinegar, raisins, salt, and pepper. Place roast on top of vegetables. Cover slow cooker with lid and cook as manufacturer directs on low setting 8 to 10 hours (or on high setting 6 to 6½ hours) or until roast is very tender.

2   Place roast on warm platter. Skim and discard fat from cooking liquid. Serve roast with vegetables and sauce.

EACH SERVING: ABOUT 360 CALORIES | 25G PROTEIN | 17G CARBOHYDRATE | 21G TOTAL FAT (8G SATURATED) | 2G FIBER | 83MG CHOLESTEROL | 540MG SODIUM

BLT BURGERS

GRILL Jazz up the classic burger with another all-American combo—
the BLT. This recipe also works well with ground chicken. Just add
salt and pepper, about ¼ teaspoon of each, before shaping the meat
into burgers. For photo, see page 52.

ACTIVE TIME: 15 MINUTES · **TOTAL TIME:** 25 MINUTES

MAKES: 4 SERVINGS

½ CUP KETCHUP

¼ CUP LIGHT MAYONNAISE

1 TABLESPOON YELLOW MUSTARD

1¼ POUNDS GROUND BEEF CHUCK

8 SLICES BACON

4 SESAME-SEED BUNS, SPLIT AND
TOASTED

SWEET ONION SLICES, TOMATO SLICES,
AND ROMAINE LETTUCE LEAVES

1 Prepare grill for direct grilling over medium heat.

2 In bowl, with fork, stir ketchup, mayonnaise, and mustard until blended;
set sauce aside. Makes about ½ cup.

3 Shape ground beef into four ¾-inch-thick burgers, handling meat as
little as possible. Wrap each burger with 2 strips bacon, arranged perpen-
dicular to each other.

4 Place burgers on grill over medium heat and grill, turning once, 10 to 12
minutes for medium or until desired doneness.

5 Serve burgers on buns with onion, tomato, lettuce, and sauce.

EACH SERVING: ABOUT 575 CALORIES | 34G PROTEIN | 27G CARBOHYDRATE | 36G TOTAL FAT
(12G SATURATED) | 2G FIBER | 111MG CHOLESTEROL | 870MG SODIUM

MINI BURGERS

 Served with one of the Creamy Burger Toppings, these minis will deliver so much flavor no one will even think about size.

TOTAL TIME: 25 MINUTES

MAKES: 12 MINI BURGERS

1¼ POUNDS GROUND BEEF CHUCK

¾ TEASPOON SALT

½ TEASPOON GROUND BLACK PEPPER

12 MINI POTATO ROLLS, MINI PITAS, OR OTHER SMALL BUNS

CHOICE OF CREAMY BURGER TOPPINGS (OPPOSITE)

PLUM TOMATO SLICES, SMALL LETTUCE LEAVES, DILL PICKLE SLICES, AND ONION SLICES (OPTIONAL)

1 Prepare grill for direct grilling over medium heat.

2 Shape beef into twelve ½-inch-thick mini burgers, handling meat as little as possible. Sprinkle both sides of burgers with salt and pepper.

3 Place mini burgers on hot grill over medium heat and grill, turning once, 5 to 6 minutes for medium or until desired doneness.

4 Serve burgers on rolls with topping of your choice and tomato, lettuce, pickles, and onion, if you like.

EACH MINI BURGER WITH ROLL: ABOUT 145 CALORIES | 10G PROTEIN | 9G CARBOHYDRATE 8G TOTAL FAT (3G SATURATED) | 1G FIBER | 32MG CHOLESTEROL | 240MG SODIUM

CREAMY BURGER TOPPINGS

   Nowadays, you can find a wide variety of commercially prepared sauces, salsas, and condiments in almost every supermarket, but, of course, nothing beats homemade. If you want to offer something a little more special than mustard, relish, and ketchup, here are three tasty mayonnaise-based toppings you can whip up in just a few minutes.

HORSERADISH-MUSTARD MAYO

In small serving bowl, combine **¼ cup light mayonnaise, 1 tablespoon undrained bottled white horseradish,** and **2 teaspoons Dijon mustard with seeds**; stir until blended. Makes about ⅓ cup.

EACH TABLESPOON: ABOUT 45 CALORIES | 0G PROTEIN | 1G CARBOHYDRATE | 4G TOTAL FAT (1G SATURATED) | 0G FIBER | 4MG CHOLESTEROL | 105MG SODIUM

BACON-CHIPOTLE MAYO

Place **2 slices bacon** on paper-towel-lined microwave-safe plate. Cover with paper towel and cook in microwave oven on High until well browned, 1½ to 2 minutes. Set aside until cool and crisp, then crumble bacon into small serving bowl. Add **¼ cup light mayonnaise** and **1 teaspoon puree from canned chipotle chile in adobo**; stir until blended. Makes about ⅓ cup.

EACH TABLESPOON: ABOUT 55 CALORIES | 1G PROTEIN | 1G CARBOHYDRATE | 5G TOTAL FAT (1G SATURATED) | 0G FIBER | 6MG CHOLESTEROL | 135MG SODIUM

ONION-THYME MAYO

Place **1 medium onion,** cut crosswise into ½-inch-thick rounds, on grill over medium heat and grill, turning once, until tender and browned on both sides, 8 to 10 minutes. Transfer onion to cutting board; coarsely chop. Place onion in small serving bowl. Add **¼ cup light mayonnaise** and **1 teaspoon fresh thyme leaves,** chopped; stir until blended. Makes about ½ cup.

EACH TABLESPOON: ABOUT 30 CALORIES | 0G PROTEIN | 2G CARBOHYDRATE | 3G TOTAL FAT (1G SATURATED) | 0G FIBER | 3MG CHOLESTEROL | 60MG SODIUM

GREEK LAMB BURGERS

**Grilling is a great way to cook juicy and flavorful ground lamb.
Try adding the chopped walnuts to the meat—they give it great
texture. If you can't find ground lamb at the supermarket, you can make
these burgers with ground beef or poultry.**

ACTIVE TIME: 20 MINUTES · **TOTAL TIME:** 25 MINUTES
MAKES: 4 SERVINGS

1 PLUM TOMATO, CHOPPED	¼ CUP WALNUTS, CHOPPED (OPTIONAL)
¼ CUP PLAIN LOW-FAT YOGURT	1 GARLIC CLOVE, CRUSHED WITH GARLIC PRESS
2 TABLESPOONS LIGHT MAYONNAISE	2 TEASPOONS GROUND CUMIN
¾ CUP LOOSELY PACKED FRESH MINT LEAVES, COARSELY CHOPPED	4 (6-INCH) PITA BREADS
1 TEASPOON SALT	1 MEDIUM KIRBY (PICKLING) CUCUMBER, NOT PEELED, SLICED
¼ TEASPOON GROUND BLACK PEPPER	
1¼ POUNDS GROUND LAMB	

1 Prepare grill for direct grilling over medium heat.

2 In small bowl, stir tomato, yogurt, mayonnaise, 2 tablespoons mint, ¼
teaspoon salt, and pepper until blended; set sauce aside. Makes about
¾ cup.

3 In medium bowl, combine lamb, walnuts (if using), garlic, cumin, remaining ¾ teaspoon salt, and remaining mint just until blended but not
overmixed.

4 Shape lamb mixture into four ¾-inch-thick burgers, handling meat as
little as possible.

5 Place burgers on grill over medium heat and grill, turning once, 10 to 12
minutes for medium or until desired doneness.

6 To serve, cut off one-third from side of each pita. Place burgers in pitas;
top with sauce and cucumber.

EACH SERVING: ABOUT 485 CALORIES | 32G PROTEIN | 31G CARBOHYDRATE | 25G TOTAL FAT
(10G SATURATED) | 3G FIBER | 105MG CHOLESTEROL | 985MG SODIUM

GINGERED PORK BURGERS

GRILL Reminiscent of Peking-style pork dumpling flavors, these Asian-spiced ground pork burgers are served with soy-sauce-flavored mayonnaise. If you prefer, you can use ground chicken instead of pork, but if you do, spray the burgers with nonstick cooking spray before placing them on the grill rack.

ACTIVE TIME: 15 MINUTES · **TOTAL TIME:** 25 MINUTES
MAKES: 4 SERVINGS

¼ CUP LIGHT MAYONNAISE

1 TABLESPOON SOY SAUCE

1¼ POUNDS GROUND PORK OR CHICKEN

½ CUP LOOSELY PACKED FRESH CILANTRO LEAVES, COARSELY CHOPPED

3 GREEN ONIONS, CHOPPED

1 TABLESPOON DRY SHERRY

1 TABLESPOON FINELY CHOPPED, PEELED FRESH GINGER

1 TEASPOON ASIAN SESAME OIL

¼ TEASPOON CRUSHED RED PEPPER

¾ TEASPOON SALT

4 SESAME-SEED HAMBURGER BUNS, SPLIT AND TOASTED

1 Prepare grill for direct grilling over medium heat.

2 In cup, with fork, stir mayonnaise and soy sauce until blended; set aside. Makes about ¼ cup.

3 In medium bowl, combine pork, cilantro, green onions, sherry, ginger, sesame oil, crushed red pepper, and salt until blended but not overmixed. Shape pork mixture into four ¾-inch-thick burgers, handling meat as little as possible.

4 Place burgers on grill over medium heat and grill, turning once, 10 to 12 minutes for medium or until desired doneness. (If using chicken, spray burgers with nonstick cooking spray and grill 12 to 14 minutes.)

5 Serve burgers on buns with mayonnaise sauce.

EACH SERVING: ABOUT 475 CALORIES | 32G PROTEIN | 25G CARBOHYDRATE | 26G TOTAL FAT (8G SATURATED) | 3G FIBER | 106MG CHOLESTEROL | 1,120MG SODIUM

VEAL SCALOPPINE MARSALA

STOVE Simple, elegant, and scrumptious, this quintessential Italian dish is quick and easy to prepare. The purpose of pounding the cutlets is twofold: to tenderize the meat and to ensure even cooking.

TOTAL TIME: 25 MINUTES

MAKES: 6 SERVINGS

1	POUND VEAL CUTLETS	3	TABLESPOONS BUTTER OR MARGARINE
¼	CUP ALL-PURPOSE FLOUR	½	CUP DRY MARSALA WINE
¼	TEASPOON SALT	½	CUP CHICKEN BROTH
⅛	TEASPOON COARSELY GROUND BLACK PEPPER	1	TABLESPOON CHOPPED FRESH PARSLEY

1 With meat mallet, pound cutlets to even ⅛-inch thickness (or place veal between two sheets of plastic wrap or waxed paper and pound with rolling pin). Cut cutlets into roughly 3-inch squares. On waxed paper, combine flour, salt, and pepper; use to coat both sides of veal pieces, shaking off excess.

2 In nonstick 10-inch skillet, melt butter over medium heat. Cook veal in batches until lightly browned, 45 to 60 seconds per side, using slotted spatula to transfer pieces to warm platter as they are browned; keep warm.

3 Stir Marsala and broth into veal drippings in pan; cook until syrupy, 4 to 5 minutes, stirring until browned bits are loosened from bottom of skillet. Pour sauce over veal and sprinkle with parsley.

EACH SERVING: ABOUT 180 CALORIES | 17G PROTEIN | 5G CARBOHYDRATE | 7G TOTAL FAT (4G SATURATED) | 0G FIBER | 75MG CHOLESTEROL | 288MG SODIUM

PORK STEAK WITH PLUM GLAZE

 For this recipe, we butterfly pork tenderloin, then pound it for quick, even cooking. A meat mallet is a handy tool for this job, but a small heavy skillet or a rolling pin will work, too.

TOTAL TIME: 30 MINUTES

MAKES: 4 SERVINGS

1 PORK TENDERLOIN (1 POUND), TRIMMED	1 TABLESPOON FRESH LEMON JUICE
1 TEASPOON SALT	½ TEASPOON GROUND CINNAMON OR CHINESE FIVE-SPICE POWDER
¼ TEASPOON COARSELY GROUND BLACK PEPPER	2 GARLIC CLOVES, CRUSHED WITH GARLIC PRESS
½ CUP PLUM JAM OR PRESERVES	4 LARGE PLUMS (1 POUND), EACH CUT IN HALF AND PITTED
1 TABLESPOON BROWN SUGAR	COOKED WHITE RICE (OPTIONAL)
1 TABLESPOON GRATED, PEELED FRESH GINGER	

1 Prepare grill for covered direct grilling over medium heat, or preheat ridged grill pan over medium heat until very hot.

2 Holding knife parallel to cutting surface and against long side of tenderloin, cut pork lengthwise almost in half, being careful not to cut all the way through. Open tenderloin like a book and spread flat. With meat mallet, pound pork to even ¼-inch thickness (or place pork between two sheets of plastic wrap or waxed paper and pound with rolling pin). Cut tenderloin crosswise into 4 steaks; season with salt and pepper.

3 In small bowl, with fork, mix jam, sugar, ginger, lemon juice, cinnamon, and garlic. Brush one side of each pork steak and cut side of each plum half with plum glaze.

4 Place steaks and plums, glaze side down, on grill or in grill pan over medium heat. Cover and cook 3 minutes. Brush steaks and plums with remaining glaze; turn steaks and plums and grill until steaks are browned on both sides and just lose their pink color throughout and plums are tender, about 3 minutes longer. Serve with rice, if desired.

EACH SERVING: ABOUT 310 CALORIES | 25G PROTEIN | 42G CARBOHYDRATE | 5G TOTAL FAT (1G SATURATED) | 2G FIBER | 66MG CHOLESTEROL | 524MG SODIUM

ORANGE PORK AND ASPARAGUS STIR-FRY

STOVE
The secrets to a perfect orange pan sauce are simple: Wash and pat dry the orange first, and avoid the bitter white pith just below the peel when grating.

TOTAL TIME: 25 MINUTES

MAKES: 4 SERVINGS

2 NAVEL ORANGES	¼ TEASPOON GROUND BLACK PEPPER
1 TEASPOON OLIVE OIL	1½ POUNDS THIN ASPARAGUS, TRIMMED AND CUT IN HALF
1 PORK TENDERLOIN (12 OUNCES), TRIMMED AND THINLY SLICED ON DIAGONAL	1 GARLIC CLOVE, CRUSHED WITH GARLIC PRESS
¾ TEASPOON SALT	¼ CUP WATER

1 From 1 orange, grate 1 teaspoon peel and squeeze ¼ cup juice. Cut peel from remaining orange and set aside, then remove and discard white pith from orange. Cut orange crosswise into ¼-inch-thick slices; cut each slice into quarters.

2 In nonstick 12-inch skillet, heat ½ teaspoon oil over medium heat until hot but not smoking. Add half of pork slices and sprinkle with ¼ teaspoon salt and ⅛ teaspoon pepper. Cook, stirring frequently (stir-frying), until pork just loses its pink color, about 2 minutes. With slotted spoon, transfer pork to plate. Repeat with remaining ½ teaspoon oil, pork, ¼ teaspoon salt, and remaining ⅛ teaspoon pepper.

3 To same skillet, add asparagus, garlic, orange peel, remaining ¼ teaspoon salt, and water; cover and cook, stirring occasionally, until asparagus is tender-crisp, about 2 minutes. Return pork to skillet. Add orange juice and orange pieces; heat through, stirring often.

EACH SERVING: ABOUT 165 CALORIES | 24G PROTEIN | 8G CARBOHYDRATE | 4G TOTAL FAT (1G SATURATED) | 2G FIBER | 50MG CHOLESTEROL | 495MG SODIUM

PORK TENDERLOIN WITH ROASTED GRAPES

  If you've never had roasted grapes, try this recipe! They are absolutely delicious and a perfect match for the pork. For photo, see page 6.

ACTIVE TIME: 15 MINUTES · **TOTAL TIME:** 30 MINUTES

MAKES: 4 SERVINGS

---

1 TEASPOON FENNEL SEEDS, CRUSHED	2 TEASPOONS EXTRA-VIRGIN OLIVE OIL
½ TEASPOON SALT	3 CUPS SEEDLESS RED AND GREEN GRAPES (ABOUT 1 POUND)
½ TEASPOON COARSELY GROUND BLACK PEPPER	½ CUP CHICKEN BROTH
1 PORK TENDERLOIN (1 POUND)	

1 Preheat oven to 475°F. In cup, with fork, stir fennel seeds, salt, and pepper. Use to rub all over pork.

2 In 12-inch skillet with oven-safe handle, heat oil over medium-high heat until very hot. Add pork and cook 5 minutes, turning to brown all sides.

3 Add grapes and broth to skillet; heat to boiling. Cover and place in oven. Roast until meat thermometer inserted in center of roast reaches 150°F, 15 to 18 minutes. Internal temperature of meat will rise to 160°F upon standing. Transfer pork to warm platter.

4 Meanwhile, heat grape mixture to boiling over high heat; boil until liquid has thickened slightly, about 1 minute. Slice pork; serve with grapes and pan juices.

EACH SERVING: ABOUT 245 CALORIES | 25G PROTEIN | 22G CARBOHYDRATE | 7G TOTAL FAT (2G SATURATED) | 2G FIBER | 74MG CHOLESTEROL | 475MG SODIUM

HAM STEAK WITH CREAMY CHEESE GRITS

This brown-sugar-glazed ham steak and cheesy grits is a down-home dinner your family is sure to love. To complete the meal, serve with orange or grapefruit sections or some sautéed collard greens.

ACTIVE TIME: 10 MINUTES · **TOTAL TIME:** 25 MINUTES

MAKES: 4 SERVINGS

1¼ CUPS WHOLE MILK

1 CAN (14½ OUNCES) LOW-SODIUM CHICKEN BROTH OR VEGETABLE BROTH

¼ TEASPOON GROUND RED PEPPER (CAYENNE)

¼ TEASPOON DRIED THYME

¾ CUP QUICK-COOKING GRITS

4 OUNCES CHEDDAR CHEESE, SHREDDED (1 CUP)

1 FULLY COOKED SMOKED-HAM CENTER SLICE, ½ INCH THICK (ABOUT 1¼ POUNDS)

2 TABLESPOONS LIGHT BROWN SUGAR

GREEN ONIONS FOR GARNISH

1   In nonreactive 2-quart saucepan, whisk together milk, broth, ground red pepper, and thyme; heat to boiling over high heat. Slowly whisk grits into liquid. Reduce heat to low; cover and simmer, stirring occasionally, until mixture has thickened, 5 to 7 minutes. Remove saucepan from heat and stir in Cheddar.

2   While grits are cooking, prepare ham: Spray cast-iron or other heavy 12-inch skillet with cooking spray; heat over medium heat until very hot. Pat ham dry with paper towels. Coat both sides of ham with brown sugar. Cook ham, turning once, until glazed and heated through, about 5 minutes. To serve, arrange ham on platter with pan juices and grits. Garnish with green onions.

EACH SERVING: ABOUT 535 CALORIES | 45G PROTEIN | 33G CARBOHYDRATE | 24G TOTAL FAT (12G SATURATED) | 1G FIBER | 122MG CHOLESTEROL | 2,499MG SODIUM

SOUTHERN PEACH PORK CHOPS

GRILL This Bayou-inspired meal pairs spice-rubbed pork chops and juicy peaches, both slathered with preserves before grilling. To prevent the food from sticking, be sure to give the grill rack a thin coat of oil before you fire it up. These luscious peaches also make a great summer dessert, so add a few extra to the grill; store in an airtight container and serve on another night with vanilla ice cream.

TOTAL TIME: 25 MINUTES

MAKES: 4 SERVINGS

1   TABLESPOON CURRY POWDER

1   TABLESPOON BROWN SUGAR

1   TABLESPOON OLIVE OIL

½   TEASPOON SALT

¼   TEASPOON GROUND CINNAMON

PINCH COARSELY GROUND BLACK PEPPER

1   GARLIC CLOVE, CRUSHED WITH GARLIC PRESS

4   BONE-IN PORK LOIN CHOPS, ¾ INCH THICK (5 OUNCES EACH)

4   LARGE PEACHES, EACH CUT IN HALF AND PITTED

½   CUP PEACH OR APRICOT JAM OR PRESERVES

1   Prepare grill for direct grilling over medium heat.

2   In cup, with fork, stir curry powder, sugar, oil, salt, cinnamon, pepper, and garlic until blended; use to rub on both sides of pork chops.

3   Brush cut side of each peach half and one side of chops with some jam. Place peaches, jam side down, and chops, jam side up, on grill over medium heat; grill 5 minutes. Turn chops and peaches; brush grilled side of chops with some jam and grill 5 minutes longer.

4   Transfer peaches as they are browned to platter. Turn chops and grill until browned on outside and still slightly pink inside, 2 to 3 minutes longer. Transfer chops to platter with peaches and serve.

EACH SERVING: ABOUT 500 CALORIES | 21G PROTEIN | 49G CARBOHYDRATE | 26G TOTAL FAT (9G SATURATED) | 2G FIBER | 77MG CHOLESTEROL | 360MG SODIUM

LOW 'N' SLOW PULLED PORK

SLOW Pork shoulder blade roast is known as a cheap cut of meat. But when slow-cooked for hours in a sweet and tangy sauce, it becomes meltingly tender.

ACTIVE TIME: 20 MINUTES · **SLOW COOK:** 8 HOURS ON LOW

MAKES: 12 SERVINGS

1 MEDIUM ONION, CHOPPED	1½ TEASPOONS SALT
½ CUP KETCHUP	1¼ TEASPOONS GROUND BLACK PEPPER
⅓ CUP CIDER VINEGAR	4 POUNDS BONELESS PORK SHOULDER BLADE ROAST (FRESH PORK BUTT), CUT INTO 4 PIECES
¼ CUP PACKED BROWN SUGAR	
¼ CUP TOMATO PASTE	12 SOFT SANDWICH BUNS OR CIABATTA ROLLS, WARMED
2 TABLESPOONS SWEET PAPRIKA	
2 TABLESPOONS WORCESTERSHIRE SAUCE	DILL PICKLES (OPTIONAL)
	POTATO CHIPS (OPTIONAL)
2 TABLESPOONS YELLOW MUSTARD	HOT SAUCE (OPTIONAL)

1 In 4½- to 6-quart slow-cooker pot, stir onion, ketchup, vinegar, brown sugar, tomato paste, paprika, Worcestershire, mustard, salt, and pepper until combined. Add pork to sauce mixture and turn to coat well with sauce.

2 Cover slow cooker with lid and cook pork mixture on Low as manufacturer directs, 8 to 10 hours or until pork is very tender.

3 With tongs, transfer pork to large bowl. Turn setting on slow cooker to High; cover and heat sauce to boiling to thicken and reduce slightly.

4 While sauce boils, with 2 forks, pull pork into shreds. Return shredded pork to slow cooker and toss with sauce to combine. Cover slow cooker and heat through on High if necessary.

5 Spoon pork mixture onto bottom of sandwich buns; replace tops of buns. Serve sandwiches with pickles, potato chips, and hot sauce, if you like.

EACH SERVING: ABOUT 475 CALORIES | 31G PROTEIN | 29G CARBOHYDRATE | 26G TOTAL FAT (9G SATURATED) | 2G FIBER | 107MG CHOLESTEROL | 760MG SODIUM

PORK CHOPS WITH PEPPERS AND ONIONS

 Juicy pork loin chops are served on a bed of colorful sautéed red peppers and green onions. For even more vibrant color, substitute a yellow or orange pepper for one of the red peppers.

ACTIVE TIME: 25 MINUTES · **TOTAL TIME:** 30 MINUTES

MAKES: 4 SERVINGS

4   BONELESS PORK LOIN CHOPS, ½ INCH THICK (4 OUNCES EACH), TRIMMED

½   TEASPOON SALT

¼   TEASPOON GROUND BLACK PEPPER

2   TEASPOONS OLIVE OIL

1   BUNCH GREEN ONIONS, GREEN TOPS CUT ON DIAGONAL INTO 3-INCH PIECES, WHITE BOTTOMS THINLY SLICED CROSSWISE

2   MEDIUM RED PEPPERS, CUT INTO 1½-INCH PIECES

1   GARLIC CLOVE, CRUSHED WITH GARLIC PRESS

⅛   TEASPOON CRUSHED RED PEPPER

½   CUP CHICKEN BROTH

1   Heat nonstick 12-inch skillet over medium heat until hot but not smoking. Add pork chops and sprinkle with salt and pepper. Cook, turning once, until lightly browned on outside and still slightly pink on inside, about 8 minutes. Transfer chops to plate; keep warm.

2   Add oil and green onion tops to skillet; cook 4 minutes. With slotted spoon, transfer green onion tops to small bowl.

3   In same skillet, add red peppers and green onion bottoms and cook, stirring occasionally, 8 minutes. Add garlic and crushed red pepper, and cook, stirring, 1 minute. Stir in broth and half of green onion tops; heat through.

4   To serve, transfer pepper mixture to platter; top with chops and remaining green onion tops.

EACH SERVING: ABOUT 210 CALORIES | 26G PROTEIN | 7G CARBOHYDRATE | 8G TOTAL FAT (2G SATURATED) | 2G FIBER | 71MG CHOLESTEROL | 495MG SODIUM

FISH & SHELLFISH

Steamed Scrod Fillets (page 95)

THAI SHRIMP AND ASPARAGUS

 STOVE **Here's a light and creamy Asian-inspired dish that comes together in minutes.**

TOTAL TIME: 15 MINUTES

MAKES: 4 SERVINGS

1 POUND SHELLED AND DEVEINED SHRIMP	1 CAN (13½ TO 14 OUNCES) LIGHT COCONUT MILK
4 TEASPOONS GREEN CURRY PASTE	2 TABLESPOONS LOW-SODIUM ASIAN FISH SAUCE (NAM PLA OR NUOC NAM, SEE TIP, PAGE 130)
1 TABLESPOON VEGETABLE OIL	
1 POUND ASPARAGUS, CUT IN 2-INCH PIECES	2 PACKAGES (8 TO 9 OUNCES EACH) PRECOOKED WHOLE-GRAIN BROWN RICE, PREPARED AS LABEL DIRECTS
3 TABLESPOONS WATER	
2 LIMES	

1 In medium bowl, toss shrimp with curry paste to coat. In 12-inch skillet, heat oil on medium-high. Add shrimp; cook 3 minutes or just until pink, stirring. Transfer to large bowl.

2 To same skillet, add asparagus and water; cook 4 minutes or until asparagus is tender-crisp and water evaporates, stirring often. From 1 lime, grate 1 teaspoon peel; cut remaining lime into 4 wedges.

3 Add asparagus to shrimp in bowl. To skillet, add coconut milk and lime peel; heat to boiling on high. Reduce heat to medium and cook 5 minutes or until slightly thickened.

4 Return shrimp mixture to skillet. Stir in fish sauce; heat through. Serve shrimp with rice and lime wedges.

EACH SERVING: ABOUT 470 CALORIES | 31G PROTEIN | 44G CARBOHYDRATE | 18G TOTAL FAT (7G SATURATED) | 3G FIBER | 172MG CHOLESTEROL | 725MG SODIUM

GRILLED SHRIMP WITH BLACK BEANS

 This twenty-minute shrimp dish is seasoned with just the right mix of fresh lime, cilantro, and jalapeño pepper.

TOTAL TIME: 20 MINUTES

MAKES: 4 SERVINGS

3 LIMES

2 CANS (15 TO 19 OUNCES EACH) BLACK BEANS, RINSED AND DRAINED (SEE TIP)

2 RIPE PLUM TOMATOES (8 OUNCES), CHOPPED

2 GREEN ONIONS, THINLY SLICED

1 SMALL YELLOW PEPPER, SEEDED AND CHOPPED

1 JALAPEÑO CHILE, SEEDED AND FINELY CHOPPED

½ CUP LOOSELY PACKED FRESH CILANTRO LEAVES, CHOPPED

1 TABLESPOON OLIVE OIL

¾ TEASPOON SALT

1 POUND LARGE SHRIMP, SHELLED AND DEVEINED, TAIL PART OF SHELL LEFT ON, IF YOU LIKE

1   Prepare grill for direct grilling over medium-high heat.

2   Meanwhile, from 1 lime, grate ½ teaspoon peel and squeeze 2 tablespoons juice. Cut remaining limes into wedges and set aside. In large bowl, stir lime juice and ¼ teaspoon lime peel with beans, tomatoes, green onions, yellow pepper, jalapeño, cilantro, oil, and ½ teaspoon salt. Set aside at room temperature. Makes about 5 cups.

3   In medium bowl, toss shrimp with remaining ¼ teaspoon lime peel and ¼ teaspoon salt. Place shrimp on grill over medium-high heat and grill, turning once, until opaque throughout, 3 to 4 minutes.

4   Stir about one-half of shrimp into bean salad; top with remaining shrimp. Serve with lime wedges.

TIP Whenever you use canned beans, always give them a quick rinse under cold water and drain them. This refreshes their flavor and removes some of the sodium added during the canning process.

EACH SERVING: ABOUT 290 CALORIES | 31G PROTEIN | 41G CARBOHYDRATE | 5G TOTAL FAT (1G SATURATED) | 14G FIBER | 180MG CHOLESTEROL | 890MG SODIUM

SHRIMP AND TOMATO SUMMER SALAD

 Want to enjoy this light but satisfying dinner salad year-round? Substitute in plum tomatoes or use 1½ pints cherry tomatoes.

TOTAL TIME: 25 MINUTES

MAKES: 6 SERVINGS

2   TABLESPOONS OLIVE OIL

2   TABLESPOONS RED WINE VINEGAR

¾   TEASPOON SALT

¼   TEASPOON COARSELY GROUND BLACK PEPPER

½   CUP LOOSELY PACKED FRESH PARSLEY LEAVES, CHOPPED

¼   CUP LOOSELY PACKED FRESH MINT LEAVES, THINLY SLICED

1   POUND COOKED, SHELLED, AND DEVEINED LARGE SHRIMP

2½ POUNDS RIPE TOMATOES (4 LARGE), CUT INTO 1-INCH PIECES

1   ENGLISH (SEEDLESS) CUCUMBER OR 4 KIRBY CUCUMBERS, CUT LENGTHWISE INTO QUARTERS, THEN CUT CROSSWISE INTO 1-INCH PIECES

1   SMALL RED ONION, CHOPPED

2   OUNCES FETA CHEESE, CRUMBLED (ABOUT ½ CUP)

In serving bowl, with wire whisk, mix oil, vinegar, salt, and pepper until blended; stir in parsley and mint. Add shrimp, tomatoes, cucumber, and onion to dressing in bowl; stir to combine. Sprinkle salad with feta and serve at room temperature, or cover and refrigerate to serve later.

EACH SERVING: ABOUT 200 CALORIES | 20G PROTEIN | 13G CARBOHYDRATE | 8G TOTAL FAT (2G SATURATED) | 3G FIBER | 156MG CHOLESTEROL | 585MG SODIUM

CITRUS SHRIMP WITH WHOLE-WHEAT COUSCOUS

STOVE Adding fruit to savory dishes creates a whole new taste dimension. In this recipe we flavor the shrimp with freshly grated orange peel and juice and extend the theme by adding orange slices to the couscous. Substitute half a coarsely chopped red or yellow pepper for the peas, if you prefer.

TOTAL TIME: 20 MINUTES

MAKES: 4 SERVINGS

3	NAVEL ORANGES	1	TABLESPOON OLIVE OIL
1½	CUPS WATER	1	POUND LARGE SHRIMP, SHELLED AND DEVEINED, TAIL PART OF SHELL LEFT ON, IF YOU LIKE
1	CUP WHOLE-WHEAT COUSCOUS (MOROCCAN PASTA)		
½	TEASPOON SALT	1	CUP FROZEN PEAS, THAWED
¼	TEASPOON GROUND BLACK PEPPER	2	TABLESPOONS FINELY CHOPPED RED ONION

1   From 1 orange, grate 1 teaspoon peel and squeeze ½ cup juice. Peel remaining 2 oranges; cut each orange crosswise into thin slices, then cut each slice in half. Set aside.

2   In 1-quart saucepan, heat water to boiling over high heat. Stir in couscous, salt, and ⅛ teaspoon pepper. Cover saucepan and remove from heat; let stand 5 minutes.

3   Meanwhile, in nonstick 12-inch skillet, heat oil over medium heat until very hot but not smoking. Stir in shrimp, orange peel and juice, and remaining ⅛ teaspoon pepper. Cook shrimp, stirring occasionally, until opaque throughout, 3 to 4 minutes.

4   With fork, fluff couscous; transfer to large bowl. Stir in peas, onion, and reserved orange slices. Serve couscous with shrimp.

EACH SERVING: ABOUT 405 CALORIES | 30G PROTEIN | 61G CARBOHYDRATE | 6G TOTAL FAT (1G SATURATED) | 11G FIBER | 140MG CHOLESTEROL | 470MG SODIUM

5 IDEAS FOR...FROZEN COOKED SHRIMP

It's the country's most popular seafood—and probably your family's favorite too. Next time you see a special on bags of frozen shrimp in your supermarket, pick up a couple and have fun with these variations. Our recipes call for either a half or whole 1-pound package of frozen, shelled, and deveined cooked shrimp. (Look for a brand that doesn't have the shell on the tail part of the shrimp.) Thaw, drain, and pat dry with paper towels, and you're ready to go.

Shrimp Quesadillas: In bowl, toss 2 cups shredded pepper Jack cheese with ⅓ cup chopped fresh cilantro and 1 teaspoon chili powder. Scatter ½ pound chopped shrimp over 4 (8-inch) flour tortillas. Top each with cheese and another tortilla. Cook in hot, nonstick 12-inch skillet over medium heat until golden on both sides, 4 minutes. Makes 4 servings.

Shrimp and Rice: In microwave-safe bowl, put 1½ cups frozen shelled edamame. Cook on High to heat through, 2 minutes. Remove; stir in 8- to 9-ounce package precooked brown rice, 1 pound shrimp, 3 sliced green onions, and ½ cup ginger-soy salad dressing. Makes 4 servings.

Lemony Bow Ties and Shrimp: Cook ½ pound bow tie pasta; drain over 1 pound shrimp set in colander. In bowl, toss pasta mixture with 1 pint halved cherry tomatoes, 1 cup chopped fresh basil, 1 tablespoon olive oil, 1 teaspoon grated fresh lemon peel, and 2 tablespoons fresh lemon juice. Makes 4 servings.

Mango Shrimp Salad: In bowl, stir ¼ cup mango chutney with ½ teaspoon grated fresh lime peel and 2 tablespoons fresh lime juice. Toss with 1 pound shrimp, 1 diced mango, and ¼ cup chopped fresh mint. Makes 4 first-course servings.

Shrimp Bruschetta: Cut 16 (½-inch thick) diagonal slices from loaf of French bread; toast until golden on both sides. In bowl, toss ¾ cup corn-and-black-bean salsa with ½ pound chopped shrimp and 3 tablespoons fresh cilantro. Spread on toasts. Makes 8 first-course servings.

SEARED SCALLOPS WITH SAFFRON COUSCOUS

Spicy chorizo accentuates the sweetness of scallops in this saffron-scented dish. Serve with a side of steamed asparagus.

TOTAL TIME: 30 MINUTES

MAKES: 4 SERVINGS

---

1   LARGE LEMON

1   BOTTLE (8 OUNCES) CLAM JUICE

¼   CUP WATER

½   CUP GRAPE TOMATOES, EACH CUT IN HALF

1   OUNCE FULLY COOKED CHORIZO, CUT LENGTHWISE IN HALF, THEN CROSSWISE INTO ¼-INCH-THICK PIECES (ABOUT ¼ CUP)

¼   TEASPOON SAFFRON THREADS, CRUMBLED (SEE TIP)

1   PACKAGE (10 OUNCES) FROZEN PEAS

1   CUP COUSCOUS (MOROCCAN PASTA)

½   TEASPOON SALT

1   POUND SEA SCALLOPS

¼   TEASPOON COARSELY GROUND BLACK PEPPER

1   TABLESPOON OLIVE OIL

1   From lemon, grate 2 teaspoons peel and squeeze 2 tablespoons juice.

2   In 3-quart saucepan, heat clam juice, water, tomatoes, chorizo, and saffron to boiling over high heat. Stir in peas; return to boiling. Remove saucepan from heat; stir in couscous, 1 teaspoon lemon peel, and ¼ teaspoon salt. Cover and let stand 5 minutes.

3   Meanwhile, pull tough crescent-shaped muscle, if any, from side of each scallop. Pat scallops dry with paper towels. In medium bowl, toss scallops with pepper and remaining ¼ teaspoon salt and 1 teaspoon lemon peel.

4   In 12-inch skillet, heat oil over medium-high heat until very hot. Add scallops; cook, turning once, until browned and opaque throughout, 5 to 6 minutes.

5   Remove skillet from heat; stir in lemon juice. Fluff couscous mixture with fork and serve with scallops.

TIP Saffron, which is used to flavor a variety of Mediterranean dishes, has a fabulous earthy flavor with a subtle bite. It's available as threads or as powder. Thread saffron, while pricey, is best; you won't need to use much.

EACH SERVING: ABOUT 400 CALORIES | 31G PROTEIN | 50G CARBOHYDRATE | 8G TOTAL FAT (2G SATURATED) | 6G FIBER | 44MG CHOLESTEROL | 790MG SODIUM

FISH TACOS

 STOVE **Ready-to-use ingredients, such as shredded cabbage mix and bottled salsa, help you get this Mexican-style meal on the table in just 15 minutes.**

TOTAL TIME: 15 MINUTES

MAKES: 4 SERVINGS

---

2 LIMES

4 CUPS SHREDDED CABBAGE MIX FOR COLESLAW (16-OUNCE BAG)

½ CUP REDUCED-FAT SOUR CREAM

1 TABLESPOON OLIVE OIL

1¼ POUNDS TILAPIA FILLETS

¼ TEASPOON GROUND CHIPOTLE CHILE

¼ TEASPOON SALT

8 CORN TORTILLAS

1 CUP FRESH SALSA

1   From limes, grate 2 teaspoons peel and squeeze ¼ cup juice.

2   In large bowl, combine coleslaw mix and lime juice; set aside. In small bowl, stir lime peel into sour cream; set aside.

3   In 12-inch skillet, heat oil on medium-high until hot. On sheet of waxed paper, sprinkle tilapia fillets with chipotle and salt to season both sides. Add fish to skillet and cook 5 to 6 minutes or until it turns opaque through-out, turning over once. Meanwhile, warm tortillas.

4   To serve, cut fillets into 8 pieces. Place 2 pieces tilapia in each tortilla; top with slaw, lime sour cream, and salsa.

EACH SERVING: ABOUT 360 CALORIES | 28G PROTEIN | 37G CARBOHYDRATE | 12G TOTAL FAT (3G SATURATED) | 4G FIBER | 12MG CHOLESTEROL | 790MG SODIUM

STEAMED SCROD FILLETS

STOVE

These fresh fillets are steamed on a bed of bok choy and carrots with a drizzle of a ginger-soy mixture. For photo, see page 84.

ACTIVE TIME: 15 MINUTES · TOTAL TIME: 25 MINUTES

MAKES: 4 SERVINGS

3 TABLESPOONS REDUCED-SODIUM SOY SAUCE

2 TABLESPOONS SEASONED RICE VINEGAR

1 TABLESPOON FINELY CHOPPED, PEELED FRESH GINGER

1 GARLIC CLOVE, CRUSHED WITH GARLIC PRESS

1 POUND BOK CHOY, COARSELY CHOPPED

1¾ CUPS SHREDDED CARROTS

4 SCROD FILLETS (6 OUNCES EACH)

3 GREEN ONIONS, SLICED

1 In small bowl, with fork, mix soy sauce, vinegar, ginger, and garlic.

2 In 12-inch skillet, toss bok choy and carrots. Fold thin ends of scrod fillets under to create even thickness. Place scrod on top of vegetables. Pour soy-sauce mixture over scrod and sprinkle with green onions; cover and heat to boiling over high heat. Reduce heat to medium; cook until scrod is just opaque throughout, about 10 minutes.

EACH SERVING: ABOUT 200 CALORIES | 34G PROTEIN | 12G CARBOHYDRATE | 2G TOTAL FAT (0G SATURATED) | 3G FIBER | 73MG CHOLESTEROL | 820MG SODIUM

TERIYAKI SALMON WITH GINGERY CHARD

STOVE For a fast weeknight dinner that looks like restaurant fare, grill salmon on the stovetop, pair with a side of Swiss chard, then drizzle with a luscious teriyaki sauce.

TOTAL TIME: 25 MINUTES

MAKES: 4 SERVINGS

1½	POUNDS RED, YELLOW, AND/OR ORANGE SWISS CHARD (SEE TIP)	1	TABLESPOON OLIVE OIL OR CANOLA OIL
3	TABLESPOONS TERIYAKI SAUCE	2	GARLIC CLOVES, CRUSHED WITH SIDE OF CHEF'S KNIFE
2	TABLESPOONS THINLY SLICED GREEN ONION	1	TEASPOON GRATED, PEELED FRESH GINGER
2	TABLESPOONS COARSELY CHOPPED FRESH CILANTRO LEAVES	¼	TEASPOON SALT
4	SALMON FILLETS, 1 INCH THICK (6 OUNCES EACH), WITH SKIN	⅛	TEASPOON GROUND BLACK PEPPER

1   Rinse chard; drain but do not spin dry. Thinly slice stems; cut leaves into 1-inch-wide pieces. Set aside.

2   In cup, combine teriyaki sauce, green onion, and cilantro; set aside.

3   Spray ridged grill pan with nonstick cooking spray; heat over medium-high heat until very hot but not smoking. Add salmon, skin side down; cook 5 minutes. Turn and cook until just opaque throughout, 3 to 4 minutes longer.

4   Meanwhile, in nonstick 12-inch skillet, heat oil over medium heat until hot. Add garlic and cook, stirring constantly, until golden, about 1 minute. Add chard in batches, then add ginger, salt, and pepper and cook, stirring frequently (stir-frying), until chard is tender, about 5 minutes.

5   To serve, transfer salmon and chard to 4 dinner plates. Drizzle salmon with teriyaki mixture.

TIP Wash the large crinkly leaves of Swiss chard with care. Fill a very large bowl or clean pot with cold water, immerse the chard leaves, and swish them around a few times, then remove them, allowing the grit to settle on the bottom. Repeat, if necessary, until the leaves are completely clean.

EACH SERVING: ABOUT 320 CALORIES | 38G PROTEIN | 9G CARBOHYDRATE | 15G TOTAL FAT (2G SATURATED) | 3G FIBER | 96MG CHOLESTEROL | 1,055MG SODIUM

ROASTED SALMON WITH SUMMER SQUASH

  Salmon paired with tarragon-tossed seasonal veggies makes for a healthy, feed-'em-fast supper—the fish roasts to perfection in just fifteen minutes. For photo, see page 2.

ACTIVE TIME: 15 MINUTES · TOTAL TIME: 30 MINUTES

MAKES: 4 SERVINGS

1 LARGE LEMON	4 MEDIUM (8 OUNCES EACH) SUMMER SQUASH (ZUCCHINI AND YELLOW), EACH CUT DIAGONALLY INTO ½-INCH-THICK SLICES
4 PIECES (6 OUNCES EACH) SKINLESS SALMON FILLET	
½ TEASPOON SALT	
¼ TEASPOON GROUND BLACK PEPPER	1 TABLESPOON CHOPPED FRESH TARRAGON LEAVES, PLUS ADDITIONAL SPRIGS FOR GARNISH

1 Preheat oven to 400°F. From lemon, grate ½ teaspoon peel and squeeze 3 tablespoons juice.

2 Place salmon in 13" by 9" glass or ceramic baking dish. Sprinkle with lemon peel, 1 tablespoon lemon juice, ¼ teaspoon salt, and ⅛ teaspoon pepper. Roast salmon 14 to 16 minutes or until just opaque throughout.

3 Meanwhile, in 4-quart saucepan, place steamer basket and 1 *inch* water. Heat water to boiling over high. Add squash; cover and reduce heat to medium. Steam vegetables 8 minutes or until tender. Transfer to medium bowl and toss with chopped tarragon, remaining ¼ teaspoon salt, remaining ⅛ teaspoon pepper, and remaining 2 tablespoons lemon juice. Arrange squash and salmon on dinner plates; garnish salmon with tarragon sprigs.

EACH SERVING: ABOUT 275 CALORIES | 27G PROTEIN | 8G CARBOHYDRATE | 11G TOTAL FAT (2G SATURATED) | 3G FIBER | 93MG CHOLESTEROL | 375MG SODIUM

JERK HALIBUT STEAK WITH SWEET-POTATO WEDGES

  Jerk seasoning, a lively blend of dry spices that originated in Jamaica, is used here to pep up halibut steaks.

ACTIVE TIME: 25 MINUTES · **TOTAL TIME:** 30 MINUTES
MAKES: 4 SERVINGS

2   POUNDS SWEET POTATOES (2 LARGE), NOT PEELED

2   GREEN ONIONS, FINELY CHOPPED

1   JALAPEÑO CHILE, SEEDED AND CHOPPED

2   TABLESPOONS FRESH LIME JUICE

2   TABLESPOONS WORCESTERSHIRE SAUCE

1   TABLESPOON GRATED, PEELED FRESH GINGER

1   TEASPOON DRIED THYME

1   TEASPOON GROUND ALLSPICE

2   TABLESPOONS OLIVE OIL

3/8   TEASPOON GROUND RED PEPPER (CAYENNE)

1/2   TEASPOON SALT

4   HALIBUT STEAKS, 1 INCH THICK (6 OUNCES EACH)

LIME WEDGES (OPTIONAL)

1   Lightly grease grill rack. Prepare grill for direct grilling over medium heat.

2   Cut each sweet potato lengthwise in half. Place on microwave-safe plate and cook in microwave oven on High, rearranging sweet potatoes halfway through cooking, until almost fork-tender, about 8 minutes.

3   Meanwhile, in medium bowl, combine green onions, jalapeño, lime juice, Worcestershire, ginger, thyme, allspice, 1 tablespoon oil, ¼ teaspoon ground red pepper, and ¼ teaspoon salt. Add halibut steaks, turning to coat. Let stand 5 minutes.

4   Cut each sweet-potato half into 4 wedges. In another medium bowl, toss sweet potatoes with remaining ¼ teaspoon salt, 1 tablespoon oil, and ⅛ teaspoon ground red pepper until evenly coated.

5   Place halibut and sweet potatoes on grill over medium heat. Spoon half of marinade over halibut; discard remaining marinade. Grill sweet-potato wedges, turning once, until tender and lightly charred, 6 to 7 minutes. Grill halibut, turning once, until just opaque throughout, 8 to 10 minutes. Transfer halibut to platter with sweet potatoes. Serve with lime wedges, if you like.

EACH SERVING: ABOUT 410 CALORIES | 38G PROTEIN | 42G CARBOHYDRATE | 9G TOTAL FAT (1G SATURATED) | 5G FIBER | 54MG CHOLESTEROL | 390MG SODIUM

ALMOND-CRUSTED TILAPIA

  Appealingly lean and with no fishy taste, mild-mannered tilapia still offers plenty of heart-healthy omega-3 fats. (Bonus: It is one of the least mercury-laden fish and is low in sodium.) Green beans and mushrooms deliver fiber, while crunchy almonds boast antioxidants.

OVEN   STOVE

TOTAL TIME: 25 MINUTES

MAKES: 4 SERVINGS

2 LEMONS	1 SMALL ONION, CHOPPED
2 TABLESPOONS OLIVE OIL	1 BAG (12 OUNCES) TRIMMED FRESH GREEN BEANS
½ TEASPOON SALT	
¼ TEASPOON COARSELY GROUND BLACK PEPPER	1 PACKAGE (10 OUNCES) SLICED WHITE MUSHROOMS
4 TILAPIA FILLETS (6 OUNCES EACH)	2 TABLESPOONS WATER
¼ CUP SLICED NATURAL ALMONDS (WITH BROWN SKIN STILL ON)	

1 Preheat oven to 425°F. From 1 lemon, grate 1 teaspoon peel and squeeze 3 tablespoons juice; cut second lemon into wedges. In cup, mix lemon peel and 1 tablespoon juice, 1 tablespoon oil, ¼ teaspoon salt, and ⅛ teaspoon pepper.

2 Spray 13" by 9" glass baking dish with nonstick spray; place tilapia, dark side down, in dish. Drizzle tilapia with lemon mixture; press almonds on top. Bake 15 minutes or until tilapia turns opaque.

3 Meanwhile, in 12-inch skillet, heat remaining 1 tablespoon oil on medium-high 1 minute. Add onion and cook 5 to 6 minutes or until golden, stirring occasionally. Stir in green beans, mushrooms, water, and remaining ¼ teaspoon salt and ⅛ teaspoon pepper. Cook about 6 minutes or until most of liquid evaporates and green beans are tender-crisp. Toss with remaining 2 tablespoons lemon juice. Serve bean mixture and lemon wedges alongside tilapia.

EACH SERVING: ABOUT 315 CALORIES | 33G PROTEIN | 15G CARBOHYDRATE | 15G TOTAL FAT (1G SATURATED) | 5G FIBER | 0MG CHOLESTEROL | 380MG SODIUM

CHUNKY SEAFOOD STEW

  This quick-fix stew uses a can of Manhattan-style clam chowder as a base. Yukon gold potatoes, chopped cod fillets, and seasonings turn it into a warming meal.

TOTAL TIME: 25 MINUTES

MAKES: 4 SERVINGS

1 TABLESPOON OLIVE OIL

1 MEDIUM ONION, SLICED

1 GREEN PEPPER, SLICED

1 RED PEPPER, SLICED

2 YUKON GOLD OR RED POTATOES (6 OUNCES EACH), NOT PEELED

1 LIME

1 CAN (10¾ OUNCES) CONDENSED MANHATTAN-STYLE CLAM CHOWDER

¾ CUP WATER

1 POUND COD OR SCROD FILLETS, CUT INTO 1-INCH PIECES

½ CUP LOOSELY PACKED FRESH PARSLEY LEAVES, CHOPPED

1   In 12-inch skillet, heat oil over medium heat until hot. Add onion and green and red peppers, cover and cook, stirring occasionally, until soft and lightly browned, 7 to 10 minutes.

2   Meanwhile, microwave potatoes: Cut potatoes into ½-inch pieces. Place in medium microwave-safe bowl and heat in microwave oven on High just until fork-tender, about 3 minutes; set aside.

3   Cut lime lengthwise in half. Cut 1 half lengthwise into 4 wedges; set aside.

4   Stir chowder and water into pepper mixture; heat to boiling. Stir in potatoes. Place cod on top of chowder mixture; cover and cook until fish is just opaque throughout, about 3 minutes.

5   Remove skillet from heat. Squeeze juice from lime half over cod and sprinkle with parsley. Serve with lime wedges.

EACH SERVING: ABOUT 295 CALORIES | 25G PROTEIN | 37G CARBOHYDRATE | 6G TOTAL FAT (1G SATURATED) | 5G FIBER | 50MG CHOLESTEROL | 420MG SODIUM

MEDITERRANEAN SWORDFISH SALAD

 This salad is a deliciously different combination of bold flavors and contrasting textures, with crisp cucumber, juicy grape tomatoes, salty feta cheese, and the meaty grilled goodness of swordfish.

TOTAL TIME: 20 MINUTES

MAKES: 4 SERVINGS

---

3   TABLESPOONS OLIVE OIL

1   SWORDFISH STEAK, 1 INCH THICK (1¼ POUNDS)

¼   TEASPOON GROUND BLACK PEPPER

¾   TEASPOON SALT

2   TABLESPOONS FRESH LEMON JUICE

1½ TEASPOONS CHOPPED FRESH OREGANO LEAVES OR ½ TEASPOON DRIED OREGANO

1   ENGLISH (SEEDLESS) CUCUMBER (12 OUNCES), CUT INTO ½-INCH PIECES

1   PINT GRAPE OR CHERRY TOMATOES, HALVED

1⅓ OUNCES FETA CHEESE, CRUMBLED (⅓ CUP)

1   In 10-inch skillet, heat 1 tablespoon oil over medium-high heat until very hot. Pat swordfish dry with paper towels. Add swordfish to skillet. Sprinkle with pepper and ½ teaspoon salt and cook, turning once, until swordfish is browned on both sides and just opaque throughout, 10 to 12 minutes.

2   Meanwhile, in large bowl, with fork, mix lemon juice, oregano, and remaining 2 tablespoons oil and ¼ teaspoon salt.

3   When swordfish is done, with wide metal spatula, transfer to cutting board; trim and discard skin. Cut swordfish into 1-inch cubes. Add swordfish, cucumber, and tomatoes to dressing in bowl; toss gently to coat. Just before serving, sprinkle with feta.

EACH SERVING: ABOUT 315 CALORIES | 32G PROTEIN | 8G CARBOHYDRATE | 17G TOTAL FAT (5G SATURATED) | 2G FIBER | 68MG CHOLESTEROL | 720MG SODIUM

SALMON BLTS WITH LEMON-DILL MAYONNAISE

GRILL This hearty sandwich is prepared with a lemon-dill mayonnaise that goes especially well with salmon. You can also substitute an equal amount of fresh tarragon or snipped chives.

TOTAL TIME: 25 MINUTES

MAKES: 4 SERVINGS

⅓ CUP LIGHT MAYONNAISE

2 TEASPOONS CHOPPED FRESH DILL

1 TEASPOON FRESHLY GRATED LEMON PEEL

4 SALMON FILLETS, 1 INCH THICK (6 OUNCES EACH), WITH SKIN

¼ TEASPOON SALT

⅛ TEASPOON COARSELY GROUND BLACK PEPPER

8 CENTER SLICES (½-INCH-THICK) COUNTRY-STYLE BREAD

4 ROMAINE LETTUCE LEAVES

2 MEDIUM TOMATOES, CUT INTO THIN SLICES

6 SLICES FULLY COOKED BACON, EACH BROKEN IN HALF

1 Lightly grease grill rack. Prepare grill for covered direct grilling over medium heat.

2 In small bowl, stir mayonnaise, dill, and lemon peel until blended; set aside.

3 Sprinkle skinless side of salmon fillets with salt and pepper. Place salmon, skin side down, on grill over medium heat; cover grill and cook, without turning, until salmon is just opaque throughout, 10 to 12 minutes.

4 Meanwhile, place bread on grill rack with salmon and grill until lightly toasted, about 1 minute on each side. Spread lemon-dill mayonnaise on one side of each toasted bread slice. Place 1 lettuce leaf on each of 4 bread slices, folding lettuce to fit; top with 2 or 3 tomato slices.

5 When salmon is done, slide thin metal spatula between salmon flesh and skin. Lift salmon from skin and transfer to plate; discard skin. Place 1 salmon fillet on each sandwich bottom. Top each fillet with 3 pieces bacon and another bread slice; serve warm.

EACH SERVING: ABOUT 570 CALORIES | 44G PROTEIN | 41G CARBOHYDRATE | 24G TOTAL FAT (5G SATURATED) | 3G FIBER | 108MG CHOLESTEROL | 955MG SODIUM

PASTA & NOODLES

Whole-Wheat Penne Genovese (page 118)

SPAGHETTI WITH PESTO AND TOMATO-MOZZARELLA SALAD

 Pesto doesn't take that long to make from scratch, and your reward is big flavor. Combined with sweet cherry tomatoes and mozzarella, you've got a pasta version of a Caprese salad.

ACTIVE TIME: 20 MINUTES · **TOTAL TIME:** 35 MINUTES
MAKES: 6 SERVINGS

1   PACKAGE (16 OUNCES) THIN SPAGHETTI OR LINGUINE

1   LARGE BUNCH FRESH BASIL

1   SMALL GARLIC CLOVE, PEELED

5   TABLESPOONS OLIVE OIL

¾   TEASPOON SALT

½   CUP FRESHLY GRATED PARMESAN CHEESE

1½ PINTS RED AND/OR YELLOW CHERRY TOMATOES, HALVED

1   TABLESPOON RED WINE VINEGAR

¼   TEASPOON GROUND BLACK PEPPER

8   OUNCES FRESH MOZZARELLA CHEESE, CUT INTO ¾-INCH CUBES

1   In large saucepot, cook pasta as label directs.

2   Meanwhile, reserve 12 small basil leaves for garnish. From remaining basil, remove enough leaves to equal 2 cups firmly packed. Wash basil well; pat dry with paper towels. In food processor with knife blade attached, blend basil leaves, garlic, 4 tablespoons oil, and ½ teaspoon salt until smooth, stopping processor and scraping down bowl occasionally. Add Parmesan; pulse to combine. Set aside.

3   In medium bowl, mix tomatoes, vinegar, and pepper with remaining 1 tablespoon oil and remaining ¼ teaspoon salt. Gently stir in mozzarella.

4   Drain spaghetti, reserving ½ cup *cooking water*. Return spaghetti and reserved pasta cooking water to saucepot; add pesto and toss well to coat pasta. Spoon spaghetti mixture into large shallow bowl; top with tomato-mozzarella salad. Garnish with reserved basil leaves.

EACH SERVING: ABOUT 540 CALORIES | 20G PROTEIN | 63G CARBOHYDRATE | 23G TOTAL FAT (8G SATURATED) | 3G FIBER | 35MG CHOLESTEROL | 550MG SODIUM

SUMMER HERB PASTA

STOVE **This light summer pasta recipe, flavored with ricotta, feta, and fresh herbs, is as easy as it is delicious.**

ACTIVE TIME: 10 MINUTES · TOTAL TIME: 20 MINUTES

MAKES: 4 SERVINGS

1 POUND CAMPANELLE OR CORKSCREW PASTA

1 CUP PART-SKIM RICOTTA CHEESE

¼ CUP CRUMBLED FETA CHEESE

½ TEASPOON FRESHLY GRATED LEMON PEEL

¼ TEASPOON SALT

¼ TEASPOON GROUND BLACK PEPPER

½ CUP LOOSELY PACKED FRESH MINT LEAVES, CHOPPED

½ CUP LOOSELY PACKED FRESH BASIL LEAVES, CHOPPED

4 PLUM TOMATOES, CHOPPED

1 In large saucepot, cook pasta as label directs.

2 Meanwhile, in bowl, combine ricotta, feta, lemon peel, salt, and pepper.

3 Reserve ⅓ *cup cooking water*. Drain pasta and return to saucepot. Stir reserved cooking water into ricotta mixture; toss with pasta to coat. Stir in herbs and chopped tomatoes.

EACH SERVING: ABOUT 560 CALORIES | 24G PROTEIN | 94G CARBOHYDRATE | 9G TOTAL FAT (5G SATURATED) | 5G FIBER | 28MG CHOLESTEROL | 500MG SODIUM

GAZPACHO-STYLE PASTA

STOVE Classic gazpacho soup ingredients get pulsed in the food processor while the small seashell pasta cooks. Toss them together, and you have a colorful summer salad. Be sure not to overprocess the vegetables.

TOTAL TIME: 30 MINUTES

MAKES: 4 SERVINGS

---

1   PACKAGE (16 OUNCES) SMALL SHELLS OR ORECCHIETTE

1   ENGLISH (SEEDLESS) CUCUMBER (1 POUND), NOT PEELED, CUT CROSSWISE INTO 1-INCH-THICK PIECES

½   MEDIUM RED PEPPER, CUT INTO 1-INCH PIECES

½   MEDIUM YELLOW PEPPER, CUT INTO 1-INCH PIECES

½   MEDIUM RED ONION, CUT INTO 1-INCH PIECES

1   JALAPEÑO CHILE, SEEDED AND COARSELY CHOPPED

1   GARLIC CLOVE, COARSELY CHOPPED

1½ POUNDS TOMATOES (5 MEDIUM), CUT INTO ½-INCH PIECES

2   TABLESPOONS OLIVE OIL

2   TABLESPOONS SHERRY OR RED WINE VINEGAR

1½ TEASPOONS SALT

1   SMALL BUNCH FRESH PARSLEY, TOUGH STEMS TRIMMED

CUCUMBER SLICES AND CHERRY TOMATOES

---

1 In large saucepot, cook pasta as label directs.

2 Meanwhile, in food processor with knife blade attached, pulse cucumber pieces, peppers, onion, jalapeño, and garlic just until finely chopped. Do not puree.

3 In large serving bowl, toss pepper mixture, tomatoes, oil, vinegar, and salt until well mixed. Reserve 4 parsley sprigs; chop remaining parsley.

4 Drain pasta. Add pasta and chopped parsley to vegetable mixture in bowl; toss well to combine. Garnish each serving with cucumber slices, cherry tomatoes, and parsley sprigs.

EACH SERVING: ABOUT 555 CALORIES | 18G PROTEIN | 100G CARBOHYDRATE | 9G TOTAL FAT (1G SATURATED) | 8G FIBER | 0MG CHOLESTEROL | 1,045MG SODIUM

PASTA RIBBONS WITH CHUNKY VEGETABLES

Just as satisfying as lasagna, this pasta dish takes half the work and half the time.

TOTAL TIME: 25 MINUTES

MAKES: 4 SERVINGS

---

1 PACKAGE (8 TO 9 OUNCES) OVEN-READY LASAGNA NOODLES (6½" BY 3½" EACH)

1 TABLESPOON OLIVE OIL

2 MEDIUM YELLOW SUMMER SQUASH AND/OR ZUCCHINI (10 OUNCES EACH), CUT INTO ¾-INCH-THICK PIECES

1 PACKAGE (10 OUNCES) MUSHROOMS, TRIMMED AND CUT INTO HALVES, OR QUARTERS IF LARGE

2 CUPS PREPARED TOMATO-BASIL PASTA SAUCE

¼ CUP HEAVY OR WHIPPING CREAM

1 SMALL PIECE (2 OUNCES) PARMESAN CHEESE

1 In 4-quart saucepan, bring *salted water* to boiling over high heat. Add lasagna, 1 noodle at a time to avoid sticking, and cook until tender, 7 to 8 minutes.

2 Meanwhile, in nonstick 12-inch skillet, heat oil over medium heat until very hot. Add squash and mushrooms; cover skillet and cook, stirring occasionally, until vegetables are tender-crisp, 4 to 5 minutes. Add pasta sauce and cream; heat to boiling, stirring frequently.

3 Drain noodles. In warm serving bowl, toss noodles with squash mixture. With vegetable peeler, shave thin strips from Parmesan. Top pasta with Parmesan shavings.

EACH SERVING: ABOUT 515 CALORIES | 19G PROTEIN | 70G CARBOHYDRATE | 18G TOTAL FAT (7G SATURATED) | 7G FIBER | 32MG CHOLESTEROL | 770MG SODIUM

SESAME NOODLES WITH CARROTS AND CUCUMBER

Kids and grownups alike will take to this Chinese-restaurant favorite made with a peanut butter and sesame dressing spiked with orange juice. Serve warm, cold, or at room temperature.

TOTAL TIME: 15 MINUTES

MAKES: 6 SERVINGS

1   PACKAGE (16 OUNCES) SPAGHETTI

1   CUP FRESH ORANGE JUICE

¼   CUP SEASONED RICE VINEGAR

¼   CUP SOY SAUCE

¼   CUP CREAMY PEANUT BUTTER

1   TABLESPOON ASIAN SESAME OIL

1   TABLESPOON GRATED, PEELED FRESH GINGER

2   TEASPOONS SUGAR

¼   TEASPOON CRUSHED RED PEPPER

1   BAG (10 OUNCES) SHREDDED CARROTS (ABOUT 3½ CUPS)

3   KIRBY CUCUMBERS (ABOUT 4 OUNCES EACH), UNPEELED AND CUT INTO MATCHSTICK-THIN STRIPS

2   GREEN ONIONS, THINLY SLICED, PLUS 6 WHOLE GREEN ONIONS FOR GARNISH

2   TABLESPOONS SESAME SEEDS, TOASTED (OPTIONAL)

1   In large saucepot, cook pasta as label directs.

2   Meanwhile, in medium bowl, with wire whisk or fork, mix orange juice, vinegar, soy sauce, peanut butter, oil, ginger, sugar, and crushed red pepper until blended; set the sauce aside.

3   Place carrots in colander; drain pasta over carrots. Put pasta and carrots in large serving bowl and add cucumbers, sliced green onions, and peanut sauce; toss. If you like, sprinkle the pasta with sesame seeds. Garnish with whole green onions.

EACH SERVING: ABOUT 445 CALORIES | 15G PROTEIN | 76G CARBOHYDRATE | 9G TOTAL FAT (2G SATURATED) | 5G FIBER | 0MG CHOLESTEROL | 1,135MG SODIUM

GREEK LASAGNA TOSS WITH TOMATOES, SHRIMP, AND FETA

Lasagna noodles are tossed with a typical Greek medley: tomatoes, oregano, shrimp, parsley, and feta cheese. Try finishing this dish with a dash of high-quality extra-virgin olive oil to impart a fruity, spicy flavor.

TOTAL TIME: 30 MINUTES

MAKES: 4 SERVINGS

1   PACKAGE (16 OUNCES) LASAGNA
    NOODLES

2   TEASPOONS OLIVE OIL

1   MEDIUM ONION, CHOPPED

1   CAN (28 OUNCES) PLUM TOMATOES
    IN JUICE

¼   TEASPOON CRUSHED RED PEPPER

¼   TEASPOON DRIED OREGANO

1   POUND LARGE SHRIMP, SHELLED AND
    DEVEINED, WITH TAIL PART OF SHELL
    LEFT ON, IF DESIRED

¼   CUP LOOSELY PACKED FRESH PARSLEY
    LEAVES, CHOPPED

2   OUNCES FETA CHEESE, CRUMBLED
    (½ CUP), PLUS ADDITIONAL FOR
    SPRINKLING ON TOP

1   In large saucepot, cook lasagna noodles until tender, about 2 minutes longer than label directs. Drain and return to saucepot.

2   Meanwhile, in 12-inch skillet, heat oil over medium heat until hot. Add onion and cook until tender and lightly browned, 5 to 7 minutes. Stir in tomatoes with their juice, crushed red pepper, and oregano; heat to boiling over high heat, breaking up tomatoes with side of spoon. Reduce heat to medium and cook until slightly thickened, about 7 minutes. Stir in shrimp and cook until shrimp are opaque throughout, 3 to 4 minutes. Remove skillet from heat; stir in parsley and ½ cup crumbled feta.

3   Add shrimp mixture to pasta in saucepot and toss to coat. Spoon pasta mixture into large serving bowl. Sprinkle additional feta on top.

EACH SERVING: ABOUT 630 CALORIES | 37G PROTEIN | 98G CARBOHYDRATE | 9G TOTAL FAT (3G SATURATED) | 5G FIBER | 153MG CHOLESTEROL | 590MG SODIUM

CREAMY RIGATONI WITH SPINACH

 You'll love this simple toss of hot pasta, creamy ricotta, Parmesan, spinach, and sun-dried tomatoes.

STOVE

TOTAL TIME: 20 MINUTES

MAKES: 6 SERVINGS

---

1 PACKAGE (16 OUNCES) RIGATONI OR ZITI

1 PACKAGE (10 OUNCES) FROZEN CHOPPED SPINACH

1 CONTAINER (15 OUNCES) PART-SKIM RICOTTA CHEESE

¼ CUP FRESHLY GRATED PARMESAN CHEESE

10 OIL-PACKED DRIED TOMATOES, DRAINED AND FINELY CHOPPED (¼ CUP)

¾ TEASPOON SALT

1 In large saucepot, begin cooking pasta as label directs. After pasta has cooked 5 minutes, add frozen spinach to pot and cook until pasta and spinach are tender, about 10 minutes longer. Drain well, reserving ½ cup pasta water. Return pasta, spinach, and reserved pasta water to saucepot.

2 Add ricotta, Parmesan, tomatoes, and salt to pasta mixture. Toss over medium-low heat until pasta is evenly coated and heated through.

EACH SERVING: ABOUT 420 CALORIES | 21G PROTEIN | 64G CARBOHYDRATE | 9G TOTAL FAT (5G SATURATED) | 4G FIBER | 25MG CHOLESTEROL | 580MG SODIUM

4 IDEAS FOR...RICOTTA CHEESE

Italians have known it all along: This fresh, creamy cheese isn't just for lasagna. Take these fast dishes, including two desserts. They're made with part-skim ricotta—which has 41 percent less fat but no less flavor than the whole-milk variety. All but one call for a 15- to 16-ounce tub.

Orange-Ricotta Pancakes: From 1 navel orange, grate 2 teaspoons peel. Remove and discard remaining peel and white pith; cut fruit into segments. In bowl, whisk together one 15- to 16-ounce tub ricotta, 4 large eggs, and orange peel. Whisk in ½ cup all-purpose flour and ½ teaspoon baking powder. Spray 12-inch nonstick skillet with nonstick spray; heat on medium 1 minute. Drop batter by the ¼ cup into skillet, making 4 to 5 pancakes at a time. Cook 10 to 12 minutes or until golden on both sides. Serve with orange segments and maple syrup. Makes 4 servings.

Puffy Bacon-Chive Casserole: Preheat oven to 350°F. In nonstick skillet, cook 3 slices bacon on medium 5 minutes or until browned; drain. Crumble when cool. Separate 5 large eggs, placing yolks in large bowl and whites in medium bowl. Whisk yolks with bacon, one 15- to 16-ounce tub ricotta, ¼ cup grated Parmesan, 2 tablespoons snipped chives, and ¼ teaspoon each salt and ground black pepper. Add 2 more egg whites to whites in bowl, and beat on high to stiff peaks. Fold whites into ricotta mixture, one-third at a time, just until blended. Bake in greased shallow 2½-quart baking dish 30 to 35 minutes or until knife inserted in center comes out clean. Makes 6 servings.

Lemon-Ricotta Fruit Dip: In blender or mini processor, blend 1 cup ricotta with 2 tablespoons chopped candied ginger until smooth. Add ½ cup jarred lemon curd and pulse just until combined. Spoon into serving bowl and refrigerate if you like. Serve with 1 pound strawberries, hulled, and 4 cups 1-inch cubes angel food cake (about 8 ounces). Makes 1½ cups dip.

Easy Cassata Parfaits: Place 1 package (10 ounces) frozen cherries on counter for 15 minutes to thaw slightly. Meanwhile, cut 4-ounce pound cake into 1-inch cubes (2 cups). In bowl, whisk one 15- to 16-ounce tub ricotta with ⅓ cup confectioners' sugar. In 4 wine goblets or parfait glasses, layer half of each of the following: ricotta mixture, cake, cherries, and ½ cup mini chocolate chips. Repeat. Makes 4 servings.

WHOLE-WHEAT PENNE GENOVESE

An onion-flecked white bean sauté adds heft to this fresh and healthy pesto pasta dish, making it light yet satisfying. For photo, see page 106.

ACTIVE TIME: 15 MINUTES · TOTAL TIME: 30 MINUTES

MAKES: 4 SERVINGS

---

12 OUNCES WHOLE-WHEAT PENNE OR ROTINI

1½ CUPS PACKED FRESH BASIL LEAVES

1 GARLIC CLOVE

3 TABLESPOONS WATER

3 TABLESPOONS EXTRA-VIRGIN OLIVE OIL

¼ TEASPOON SALT

¼ TEASPOON GROUND BLACK PEPPER

½ CUP GRATED PARMESAN CHEESE

1 SMALL ONION (4 TO 6 OUNCES), CHOPPED

1 CAN (15 TO 19 OUNCES) WHITE KIDNEY BEANS (CANNELLINI), RINSED AND DRAINED

1 PINT GRAPE TOMATOES (RED, YELLOW, AND ORANGE MIX IF AVAILABLE), EACH CUT INTO QUARTERS

---

1   In large saucepot, cook pasta as label directs.

2   Meanwhile, make pesto: In food processor with knife blade attached, blend basil, garlic, water, 2 tablespoons oil, salt, and pepper until pureed, stopping processor occasionally and scraping bowl with rubber spatula. Add Parmesan; pulse to combine. Set aside.

3   In 12-inch skillet, heat remaining 1 tablespoon oil on medium until very hot; add onion and cook 5 to 7 minutes or until beginning to soften. Stir in white beans, and cook 5 minutes longer, stirring occasionally.

4   Reserve ¼ cup *pasta cooking water*. Drain pasta and return to saucepot; stir in white bean mixture, pesto, cut-up tomatoes, and reserved cooking water. Toss to coat.

EACH SERVING: ABOUT 560 CALORIES | 22G PROTEIN | 88G CARBOHYDRATE | 15G TOTAL FAT (3G SATURATED) | 14G FIBER | 8MG CHOLESTEROL | 652MG SODIUM

PASTA ALLA VODKA

 We use orecchiette ("little ears" in Italian) in this restaurant favorite, but penne or rotini pasta are also good options for this creamy sauce.

TOTAL TIME: 20 MINUTES

MAKES: 4 SERVINGS

---

1   PACKAGE (16 OUNCES) ORECCHIETTE OR ROTINI

1   CUP FROZEN PEAS

1   CAN (14 TO 16 OUNCES) WHOLE TOMATOES IN JUICE, DRAINED

½   CUP HEAVY OR WHIPPING CREAM

½   CUP MILK

3   TABLESPOONS VODKA (OPTIONAL)

4   TEASPOONS TOMATO PASTE

½   TEASPOON SALT

⅛ TO ¼ TEASPOON CRUSHED RED PEPPER

½   CUP LOOSELY PACKED FRESH BASIL LEAVES, THINLY SLICED

1   In large saucepot, begin cooking pasta as label directs. About 2 minutes before pasta is done, add frozen peas to pot. Cook until pasta is done; drain. Return pasta and peas to saucepot.

2   Meanwhile, chop tomatoes. In nonstick 2-quart saucepan, heat tomatoes, cream, milk, vodka (if using), tomato paste, salt, and crushed red pepper over medium-low heat just to simmering.

3   Add tomato-cream sauce to pasta in saucepot; toss until well combined. Sprinkle with basil.

EACH SERVING: ABOUT 590 CALORIES | 19G PROTEIN | 98G CARBOHYDRATE | 15G TOTAL FAT (8G SATURATED) | 4G FIBER | 45MG CHOLESTEROL | 635MG SODIUM

CHICKEN PASTA PRIMAVERA

STOVE Thanks to the addictively rich sauce thickened with cream and Parmesan cheese, your family will clamor for seconds. You'll appreciate the veggies in the dish—including a generous portion of asparagus.

ACTIVE TIME: 25 MINUTES · **TOTAL TIME:** 30 MINUTES

MAKES: 6 SERVINGS

12 OUNCES CAVATAPPI OR FUSILLI PASTA

2 GREEN ONIONS

4 TEASPOONS OLIVE OIL

1½ POUNDS SKINLESS, BONELESS CHICKEN-BREAST HALVES, CUT INTO 1-INCH CHUNKS

½ TEASPOON SALT

¼ TEASPOON GROUND BLACK PEPPER

1 GARLIC CLOVE, CRUSHED WITH PRESS

1 POUND ASPARAGUS, TRIMMED AND CUT INTO 1-INCH PIECES

1 MEDIUM RED PEPPER, THINLY SLICED

½ CUP HEAVY OR WHIPPING CREAM

¼ TEASPOON CRUSHED RED PEPPER

½ CUP FRESHLY GRATED PARMESAN CHEESE

¼ CUP LOOSELY PACKED FRESH BASIL LEAVES, THINLY SLICED

1 In large saucepot, cook pasta as label directs. Drain pasta, reserving ½ *cup pasta cooking water*. Return pasta and reserved cooking water to saucepot.

2 Meanwhile, slice green onions; reserve 2 tablespoons sliced dark green tops for garnish. In 12-inch skillet, heat 2 teaspoons oil on medium-high until hot. Sprinkle chicken with ¼ teaspoon salt and pepper. Add chicken to skillet and cook 7 minutes or until chicken is browned and no longer pink throughout, stirring occasionally. Transfer chicken to medium bowl; set aside.

3 To same skillet, add remaining 2 teaspoons oil; reduce heat to medium. Add green onions and garlic; cook 1 minute, stirring. Add asparagus and red pepper; cook 6 to 7 minutes or until vegetables are tender-crisp, stirring frequently. Stir in cream, crushed red pepper, and remaining ¼ teaspoon salt. Heat to boiling over medium-high heat. Stir in reserved chicken pieces and remove skillet from heat.

4 To saucepot with pasta, add Parmesan, chicken mixture, and basil; stir to combine. Spoon into bowls and garnish with reserved dark green onion.

EACH SERVING: ABOUT 485 CALORIES | 38G PROTEIN | 46G CARBOHYDRATE | 15G TOTAL FAT (7G SATURATED) | 3G FIBER | 98MG CHOLESTEROL | 470MG SODIUM

PENNE RIGATE WITH SWEET-AND-SPICY PICADILLO SAUCE

STOVE

This spicy-sweet spaghetti with meat sauce features picadillo: a popular Latin American dish made with ground pork and beef or veal, tomatoes, garlic, onions, raisins, and olives. You might want to double the sauce and serve the leftovers with black beans and rice.

TOTAL TIME: 25 MINUTES

MAKES: 6 SERVINGS

1   PACKAGE (16 OUNCES) PENNE RIGATE, BOW TIES, OR RADIATORE, PREFERABLY WHOLE WHEAT

2   TEASPOONS OLIVE OIL

1   SMALL ONION, FINELY CHOPPED

2   GARLIC CLOVES, CRUSHED WITH GARLIC PRESS

¼   TEASPOON GROUND CINNAMON

⅛ TO ¼ TEASPOON GROUND RED PEPPER (CAYENNE)

12   OUNCES LEAN (90%) GROUND BEEF

½   TEASPOON SALT, PLUS MORE TO TASTE

1   CAN (14 TO 15 OUNCES) WHOLE TOMATOES IN PUREE (IF NOT AVAILABLE, USE WHOLE TOMATOES IN JUICE), PREFERABLY REDUCED SODIUM

½   CUP DARK SEEDLESS RAISINS

¼   CUP CHOPPED PIMIENTO-STUFFED OLIVES (SALAD OLIVES), DRAINED

1   In large saucepot, cook pasta as label directs. Drain, reserving 1 *cup pasta water*. Return pasta to saucepot.

2   Meanwhile, in nonstick 12-inch skillet, heat olive oil over medium heat until hot. Add onion and cook, stirring frequently, until tender, about 5 minutes. Stir in garlic, cinnamon, and ground red pepper; cook 30 seconds. Add ground beef and salt and cook, stirring and breaking up meat with side of spoon, until beef begins to brown, about 5 minutes. Spoon off any excess fat as necessary. Stir in tomatoes with their puree, raisins, and olives, breaking up tomatoes with side of spoon. Cook until sauce thickens slightly, about 5 minutes longer.

3   Add ground-beef mixture and reserved pasta water to pasta in saucepot and toss until well combined. Season with salt to taste.

EACH SERVING (MADE WITH REDUCED-SODIUM TOMATOES): ABOUT 452 CALORIES

22G PROTEIN | 67G CARBOHYDRATE | 12G TOTAL FAT (3G SATURATED) | 9G FIBER

37MG CHOLESTEROL | 175MG SODIUM

FETTUCCINE WITH TURKEY BOLOGNESE

 STOVE **Wondering what to do with your leftover Thanksgiving turkey? Try stirring it into this full-flavored (and healthful!) Bolognese pasta sauce.**

TOTAL TIME: 25 MINUTES

MAKES: 6 SERVINGS

---

1 TABLESPOON OLIVE OIL	½ CUP WHOLE MILK
1 MEDIUM ONION, CHOPPED	2 CUPS CHOPPED LEFTOVER COOKED TURKEY
1 MEDIUM CARROT, CHOPPED	
1 STALK CELERY, CHOPPED	1 PACKAGE (16 OUNCES) FETTUCCINE OR LINGUINE
1 CLOVE GARLIC, CRUSHED WITH PRESS	1 CUP LOOSELY PACKED FRESH PARSLEY LEAVES, CHOPPED
1 CAN (28 OUNCES) CRUSHED TOMATOES	
¼ TEASPOON SALT	½ CUP FRESHLY GRATED PARMESAN CHEESE, PLUS ADDITIONAL FOR SERVING
¼ TEASPOON COARSELY GROUND BLACK PEPPER	

1 In 12-inch skillet, heat oil on medium until hot. Add onion, carrot, and celery; cover and cook 8 minutes or until tender, stirring occasionally. Stir in garlic and cook 1 minute. Add tomatoes, salt, and pepper; heat to boiling on medium-high. Reduce heat to low and simmer, uncovered, 10 minutes, stirring occasionally. Stir in milk and turkey; heat through.

2 While sauce is cooking, in large saucepot, cook fettuccine as label directs. Reserve 1 *cup pasta cooking water*. Drain fettuccine and return to saucepot.

3 Remove skillet from heat. Add Bolognese sauce, chopped parsley, and grated Parmesan to fettuccine in saucepot and toss to combine, adding cooking water as necessary if sauce is too thick. Spoon into warm bowls and serve with additional Parmesan.

EACH SERVING: ABOUT 490 CALORIES | 30G PROTEIN | 71G CARBOHYDRATE | 9G TOTAL FAT (3G SATURATED) | 5G FIBER | 44MG CHOLESTEROL | 710MG SODIUM

SPAGHETTI WITH SZECHUAN CHICKEN AND PEANUTS

 Pasta goes Asian with this tasty dish sparked with the delicious heat of fresh ginger.

TOTAL TIME: 25 MINUTES

MAKES: 6 SERVINGS

1   PACKAGE (16 OUNCES) WHOLE-WHEAT SPAGHETTI

1   TEASPOON VEGETABLE OIL

2   BUNCHES GREEN ONIONS, CUT INTO ½-INCH PIECES

1   POUND GROUND CHICKEN OR TURKEY BREAST MEAT

2   TABLESPOONS GRATED, PEELED FRESH GINGER

3   GARLIC CLOVES, CRUSHED WITH GARLIC PRESS

1   BAG (12 TO 16 OUNCES) SHREDDED BROCCOLI, CAULIFLOWER, CARROT, AND CABBAGE BLEND

1   CAN (14 TO 15 OUNCES) CHICKEN BROTH (1¾ CUPS)

⅓   CUP STIR-FRY SAUCE

¼   CUP CREAMY NATURAL PEANUT BUTTER

HOT PEPPER SAUCE (OPTIONAL)

1   In large saucepot, cook pasta as label directs.

2   Meanwhile, in 12-inch skillet, heat oil over high heat. Add green onions and cook until wilted, 1 to 2 minutes, stirring; transfer to bowl.

3   In same skillet over high heat, cook chicken, ginger, and garlic until chicken is no longer pink, about 3 minutes, breaking chicken up with a spoon. Stir in vegetable blend, broth, stir-fry sauce, peanut butter, and green onions; heat to boiling. Reduce heat to medium and cook until vegetables are tender-crisp and sauce thickens slightly, 6 to 8 minutes, stirring.

4   Drain spaghetti; return to saucepot. Add chicken mixture and toss to combine. Serve with hot pepper sauce, if desired.

EACH SERVING: ABOUT 475 CALORIES | 34G PROTEIN | 70G CARBOHYDRATE | 9G TOTAL FAT (1G SATURATED) | 10G FIBER | 44MG CHOLESTEROL | 580MG SODIUM

PASTA WITH RICOTTA AND GRAPE TOMATOES

A simple combination of creamy ricotta cheese, basil, and tomatoes is the secret to this flavorful, easy-to-prepare pasta. If possible, purchase the freshest basil you can find on the day you intend to use it.

TOTAL TIME: 30 MINUTES

MAKES: 4 SERVINGS

1   PACKAGE (16 OUNCES) PENNE RIGATE

1   TEASPOON OLIVE OIL

1   GARLIC CLOVE, CRUSHED WITH GARLIC PRESS

1   PINT GRAPE TOMATOES, EACH CUT IN HALF

¼   CUP CHOPPED FRESH BASIL

1   CONTAINER (15 OUNCES) PART-SKIM RICOTTA CHEESE

⅓   CUP FRESHLY GRATED PECORINO-ROMANO CHEESE

1   In large saucepot, cook pasta as label directs.

2   Meanwhile, in nonstick 10-inch skillet, heat oil over medium heat. Add garlic and tomatoes; cook, shaking pan, 5 minutes. Remove skillet from heat; stir in basil.

3   Drain pasta, reserving ½ cup cooking water. Return pasta to saucepot. Add ricotta, Romano, and reserved cooking water to pasta; toss until well combined. Top with tomato mixture.

EACH SERVING: ABOUT 580 CALORIES | 26G PROTEIN | 95G CARBOHYDRATE | 9G TOTAL FAT (4G SATURATED) | 2G FIBER | 33MG CHOLESTEROL | 335MG SODIUM

PENNE WITH SAUSAGE AND BROCCOLI RABE

 STOVE Balancing the bracing bite of broccoli rabe with the savory sweetness of Italian sausage, this Tuscan time saver will become your weekday default dinner.

TOTAL TIME: 30 MINUTES

MAKES: 4 SERVINGS

1 BUNCH BROCCOLI RABE (1 POUND)

12 OUNCES PENNE

1 LINK (4 OUNCES) SWEET ITALIAN SAUSAGE, CASING REMOVED

2 SHALLOTS, FINELY CHOPPED

2 GARLIC CLOVES, CRUSHED WITH PRESS

¼ CUP FRESHLY GRATED PARMESAN CHEESE, PLUS ADDITIONAL FOR GARNISH

¼ TEASPOON SALT

¼ TEASPOON GROUND BLACK PEPPER

1 Heat large covered saucepot of *salted water* to boiling on high. Meanwhile, trim tough stem ends from broccoli rabe and discard. Cut broccoli rabe into 1-inch pieces and add to boiling water. Cook 4 to 5 minutes or until bright green and just tender. With slotted spoon, transfer broccoli rabe to large colander, leaving water in pot on stove. Rinse broccoli rabe with cold water and drain again.

2 Return broccoli rabe cooking water to boiling and cook penne in it as label directs.

3 Meanwhile, heat deep 12-inch skillet on medium-high until hot. Add sausage in single layer; cook 4 to 5 minutes or until it browns evenly and loses its pink color. (Reduce heat to medium if sausage browns too quickly.) Add shallots and garlic; cook 2 minutes or until tender, stirring. Transfer *1½ cups pasta cooking water* from saucepot to skillet. Heat to boiling, stirring occasionally.

4 Drain pasta and add to skillet with sausage. Stir in Parmesan, broccoli rabe, salt, and pepper until well mixed. Divide among shallow bowls; sprinkle with additional Parmesan.

EACH SERVING: ABOUT 470 CALORIES | 20G PROTEIN | 70G CARBOHYDRATE | 12G TOTAL FAT (4G SATURATED) | 4G FIBER | 26MG CHOLESTEROL | 765MG SODIUM

THAI NOODLES WITH BEEF AND BASIL

 STOVE **Why spring for takeout when you can toss together a terrific noodle stir-fry for a fraction of the cost?**

TOTAL TIME: 25 MINUTES

MAKES: 4 SERVINGS

---

1 PACKAGE (7 TO 8 OUNCES) RICE STICK NOODLES	1 TEASPOON SUGAR
1 TABLESPOON VEGETABLE OIL	¾ TEASPOON CRUSHED RED PEPPER
4 GARLIC CLOVES, THINLY SLICED	¼ CUP CHOPPED FRESH CILANTRO
3-INCH PIECE FRESH GINGER, PEELED, CUT INTO THIN SLIVERS	¼ CUP SLICED FRESH BASIL
1 MEDIUM ONION, THINLY SLICED	1 SMALL CUCUMBER, CUT LENGTHWISE IN HALF AND THINLY SLICED CROSSWISE
12 OUNCES LEAN (90%) GROUND BEEF	½ CUP BEAN SPROUTS, RINSED AND DRAINED
½ CUP CHICKEN BROTH	¼ CUP UNSALTED PEANUTS, CHOPPED
3 TABLESPOONS ASIAN FISH SAUCE (NAM PLA OR NUOC NAM; SEE TIP)	1 LIME, CUT INTO WEDGES

1 In large bowl, soak rice stick noodles in enough *hot water* to cover for 15 minutes. (Do not soak longer or noodles may become too soft.) Drain.

2 Meanwhile, heat oil in 12-inch skillet over medium heat. Add garlic, ginger, and onion; cook, stirring occasionally, until golden, 8 to 10 minutes. Stir in beef; cook, stirring and breaking up beef with side of spoon, until meat is no longer pink, about 5 minutes. Stir in broth, fish sauce, sugar, and crushed red pepper; simmer, uncovered, until thickened slightly, about 5 minutes.

3 Add drained noodles, cilantro, and basil to beef mixture; cook, stirring, until heated through. Divide noodle mixture among 4 bowls; top each with cucumber, bean sprouts, and peanuts. Serve with lime wedges.

TIP Highly pungent, Asian fish sauce is made from the liquid of salted fermented anchovies. That means little goes a long way—and it has an extended shelf life. If you don't have any on hand, substitute reduced-sodium soy sauce.

EACH SERVING: ABOUT 455 CALORIES | 25G PROTEIN | 60G CARBOHYDRATE | 14G TOTAL FAT (3G SATURATED) | 4G FIBER | 40MG CHOLESTEROL | 720MG SODIUM

VEGETARIAN

Queso Blanco Soft Tacos (page 141)

FLORENTINE FRITTATA

  This frittata, which is a thin, flat pancake-style omelet from Italy, combines the smooth creaminess of mozzarella and the salty tang of feta. It is delicious hot or cold, and you can substitute any leftover cooked vegetables for the spinach and tomatoes.

ACTIVE TIME: 15 MINUTES · **TOTAL TIME:** 20 MINUTES

MAKES: 4 SERVINGS

---

1 PACKAGE (10 OUNCES) FROZEN CHOPPED SPINACH, THAWED AND SQUEEZED DRY

4 LARGE EGGS

4 LARGE EGG WHITES

2 GREEN ONIONS, THINLY SLICED

¼ CUP CRUMBLED FETA CHEESE

3 OUNCES PART-SKIM MOZZARELLA CHEESE, SHREDDED (¾ CUP)

¼ TEASPOON SALT

1 TABLESPOON OLIVE OIL

1 CUP GRAPE OR CHERRY TOMATOES

1 Preheat broiler. In large bowl, with fork, mix spinach, eggs, egg whites, green onions, feta, ½ cup mozzarella, and salt until well blended.

2 In nonstick 10-inch skillet with broiler-safe handle (if handle is not broiler-safe, wrap handle of skillet with double layer of foil), heat oil over medium heat. Pour egg mixture into skillet; arrange tomatoes on top, pushing some down. Cover skillet and cook frittata until egg mixture is just set around edge, 5 to 6 minutes.

3 Place skillet in broiler 5 to 6 inches from heat source and broil frittata until just set in center, 4 to 5 minutes. Sprinkle with remaining ¼ cup mozzarella; broil until cheese melts, about 1 minute longer.

4 To serve, loosen frittata from skillet. Serve directly from skillet or slide onto warm platter; cut into wedges.

EACH SERVING: ABOUT 230 CALORIES | 18G PROTEIN | 6G CARBOHYDRATE | 14G TOTAL FAT (6G SATURATED) | 2G FIBER | 233MG CHOLESTEROL | 570MG SODIUM

WHOLE-WHEAT PITA PIZZAS WITH VEGETABLES

  We topped whole-wheat pitas with ricotta cheese, garbanzo beans, and sautéed vegetables for a fast dinner the whole family will love.

ACTIVE TIME: 25 MINUTES · TOTAL TIME: 35 MINUTES

MAKES: 4 SERVINGS

---

1 TEASPOON OLIVE OIL

1 MEDIUM RED ONION, SLICED

2 GARLIC CLOVES, CRUSHED WITH GARLIC PRESS

¼ TEASPOON CRUSHED RED PEPPER

8 OUNCES BROCCOLI FLOWERETS (HALF 16-OUNCE BAG), CUT INTO 1½-INCH PIECES

½ TEASPOON SALT

¼ CUP WATER

1 CAN (15 TO 19 OUNCES) GARBANZO BEANS, RINSED AND DRAINED

1 CUP PART-SKIM RICOTTA CHEESE

4 (6-INCH) WHOLE-WHEAT PITA BREADS, SPLIT HORIZONTALLY IN HALF

½ CUP FRESHLY GRATED PARMESAN CHEESE

2 RIPE MEDIUM PLUM TOMATOES, CUT INTO ½-INCH CHUNKS

---

1 Preheat oven to 450°F.

2 In nonstick 12-inch skillet, heat oil over medium heat until hot. Add onion and cook until golden, 8 to 10 minutes, stirring occasionally. Add garlic and crushed red pepper, and cook 30 seconds, stirring. Add broccoli, ¼ teaspoon salt, and water; heat to boiling. Reduce heat to medium; cover and cook until broccoli is tender-crisp, about 5 minutes.

3 Meanwhile, in small bowl, with potato masher or fork, mash garbanzo beans with ricotta and remaining ¼ teaspoon salt until almost smooth.

4 Arrange pita halves on two large cookie sheets. Bake until lightly toasted, about 3 minutes.

5 Spread bean mixture on toasted pitas. Top with broccoli mixture and sprinkle with Parmesan. Bake until heated through, 7 to 10 minutes longer. Sprinkle with tomatoes to serve.

EACH SERVING: ABOUT 510 CALORIES | 27G PROTEIN | 77G CARBOHYDRATE | 13G TOTAL FAT (6G SATURATED) | 11G FIBER | 27MG CHOLESTEROL | 1,155MG SODIUM

ARTICHOKE AND GOAT CHEESE PIZZA

OVEN Delicate layers of phyllo form the crust of this rich, savory pizza. If you will be using frozen phyllo, it's best to plan ahead. Leave the unwrapped package in the refrigerator for a full day. A gradual thaw will produce sheets that are pliable and less likely to stick together or tear.

ACTIVE TIME: 10 MINUTES · **TOTAL TIME:** 25 MINUTES
MAKES: 4 SERVINGS

6   SHEETS (16" BY 12" EACH) FRESH OR FROZEN (THAWED) PHYLLO

2   TABLESPOONS BUTTER OR MARGARINE, MELTED

4   OUNCES SOFT, MILD GOAT CHEESE, SUCH AS MONTRACHET

1   JAR (6 OUNCES) MARINATED ARTICHOKE HEARTS, DRAINED AND CUT INTO PIECES

1½ CUPS GRAPE OR CHERRY TOMATOES, EACH CUT IN HALF

1   Preheat oven to 450°F. Place 1 sheet of phyllo on ungreased large cookie sheet; brush with some melted butter. Repeat layering with remaining phyllo and butter, but do not brush top layer.

2   Crumble cheese over phyllo; top with artichokes and tomatoes. Bake until golden brown around edges, 12 to 15 minutes.

3   Transfer pizza to large cutting board. With pizza cutter or knife, cut pizza lengthwise in half, then cut each half crosswise into 4 pieces.

EACH SERVING (2 PIECES): ABOUT 240 CALORIES | 9G PROTEIN | 20G CARBOHYDRATE
16G TOTAL FAT (8G SATURATED) | 2G FIBER | 28MG CHOLESTEROL | 366MG SODIUM

RICOTTA-SPINACH CALZONE

  Anybody who eats Italian food is likely to be familiar with the calzone: a large, pizza-dough turnover stuffed with meat, vegetables, and/or cheese. Refrigerated pizza dough makes calzones a snap to put together.

ACTIVE TIME: 10 MINUTES · TOTAL TIME: 30 MINUTES

MAKES: 4 SERVINGS

1 PACKAGE (10 OUNCES) FROZEN CHOPPED SPINACH

1 CUP PART-SKIM RICOTTA CHEESE

1 CUP SHREDDED MOZZARELLA CHEESE (HALF AN 8-OUNCE PACKAGE)

1 TABLESPOON CORNSTARCH

½ TEASPOON DRIED OREGANO

1 PACKAGE (10 OUNCES) REFRIGERATED PIZZA DOUGH

½ CUP PREPARED MARINARA SAUCE

1 Preheat oven to 400°F. Remove frozen spinach from package. In small microwave-safe bowl, microwave spinach on High until mostly thawed but still cool enough to handle, 2 to 3 minutes. Remove excess water (see Tip).

2 Meanwhile, in small bowl, stir ricotta, mozzarella, cornstarch, and oregano until blended; set aside.

3 Spray large cookie sheet with nonstick cooking spray. Unroll pizza dough in center of cookie sheet. With fingertips, press dough into 14" by 10" rectangle.

4 Spread cheese mixture lengthwise on half of dough, leaving 1-inch border. Spoon marinara sauce over cheese mixture; top with spinach. Fold other half of dough over filling. Pinch edges together to seal. Bake until well browned on top, 20 to 25 minutes. Cut calzone into 4 pieces to serve.

TIP For best results, be sure to remove as much moisture as possible from the almost-thawed spinach. Hold the spinach over the sink and squeeze tightly with your hands. Then, place it on a double layer of paper towels, bring up the corners to form a knot, and twist until the liquid is expelled.

EACH SERVING: ABOUT 400 CALORIES | 21G PROTEIN | 43G CARBOHYDRATE | 15G TOTAL FAT (5G SATURATED) | 4G FIBER | 19MG CHOLESTEROL | 1,055MG SODIUM

ZUCCHINI AND BEAN BURRITOS

 You can prepare these veggie and bean burritos in minutes. Canned beans and a jar of your favorite chunky-style salsa make it as easy as it is fast.

ACTIVE TIME: 10 MINUTES · TOTAL TIME: 20 MINUTES

MAKES: 4 SERVINGS

---

2 TEASPOONS VEGETABLE OIL

4 MEDIUM ZUCCHINI (8 TO 10 OUNCES EACH), EACH CUT LENGTHWISE IN HALF, THEN SLICED CROSSWISE

¼ TEASPOON SALT

¼ TEASPOON GROUND CINNAMON

1 CAN (15 OUNCES) SPANISH-STYLE RED KIDNEY BEANS

1 CAN (15 TO 19 OUNCES) BLACK BEANS, RINSED AND DRAINED

4 (10-INCH) FLOUR TORTILLAS, WARMED

4 OUNCES MONTEREY JACK CHEESE, SHREDDED (1 CUP)

½ CUP LOOSELY PACKED FRESH CILANTRO LEAVES

1 JAR (16 OUNCES) CHUNKY-STYLE SALSA

1 In nonstick 12-inch skillet, heat oil over medium-high heat until hot. Add zucchini, salt, and cinnamon and cook until zucchini is tender-crisp, about 5 minutes.

2 Meanwhile, in 2-quart saucepan, heat kidney beans with their sauce and black beans just to simmering over medium heat; keep warm.

3 To serve, allow each person to assemble burrito as desired, using a warm tortilla, zucchini, bean mixture, Monterey Jack, and cilantro. Pass salsa to serve with burritos.

EACH SERVING: ABOUT 550 CALORIES | 29G PROTEIN | 77G CARBOHYDRATE | 17G TOTAL FAT (1G SATURATED) | 19G FIBER | 25MG CHOLESTEROL | 1,943MG SODIUM

QUESO BLANCO SOFT TACOS

STOVE Queso blanco, a tangy white cheese that's firmer than mozzarella so it holds its shape when melted, is a delicious counterpoint to a mix of crisp veggies and fresh cilantro—all wrapped up in soft tortillas. For photo, see page 132.

TOTAL TIME: 20 MINUTES

MAKES: 4 SERVINGS

3   GREEN ONIONS, THINLY SLICED

3   PLUM TOMATOES, CUT INTO ½-INCH PIECES

1   RIPE AVOCADO, PITTED, PEELED, AND CUT INTO ½-INCH PIECES

¼   SMALL HEAD ROMAINE LETTUCE, THINLY SLICED (2 CUPS)

¼   CUP LOOSELY PACKED FRESH CILANTRO LEAVES

1   CUP MILD OR MEDIUM-HOT SALSA

1   PACKAGE (12 OUNCES) QUESO BLANCO (MEXICAN FRYING CHEESE; SEE TIP), CUT INTO 12 SLICES

12   (6-INCH) CORN TORTILLAS, WARMED

1   LIME, CUT INTO 4 WEDGES

1   On platter, arrange green onions, tomatoes, avocado, lettuce, and cilantro. Pour salsa into serving bowl.

2   Heat nonstick 12-inch skillet over medium heat until hot. Add cheese and heat, turning over once, until dark brown in spots, 2 to 3 minutes.

3   Place 1 slice cheese in each tortilla and fold in half. Serve immediately with vegetable platter, salsa, and lime wedge.

TIP If you can't find queso blanco in your supermarket's dairy case, use shredded Monterey Jack. Sprinkle some cheese on half of each tortilla then fold the other half over. Place the tortillas on a cookie sheet and heat in a 400°F oven until the cheese has melted, 4 to 5 minutes.

EACH SERVING: ABOUT 545 CALORIES | 26G PROTEIN | 49G CARBOHYDRATE | 29G TOTAL FAT (13G SATURATED) | 9G FIBER | 60MG CHOLESTEROL | 1,300MG SODIUM

TORTILLA PIE

OVEN Not really a pie per se, this savory main dish more closely re-
sembles a triple-decker quesadilla, with flour tortillas layered with
salsa, a black bean and corn mixture, and Monterey Jack cheese. If you
want a more authentic flavor and you have the time, prepare your own
salsa, and instead of Monterey Jack, use crumbled queso blanco,
if available (see page 141).

ACTIVE TIME: 10 MINUTES · TOTAL TIME: 20 MINUTES

MAKES: 4 SERVINGS

1 JAR (11 TO 12 OUNCES) MEDIUM-HOT
SALSA

1 CAN (8 OUNCES) NO-SALT-ADDED
TOMATO SAUCE

1 CAN (15 TO 16 OUNCES) NO-SALT-
ADDED BLACK BEANS, RINSED AND
DRAINED

1 CAN (15 TO 16 OUNCES) NO-SALT-
ADDED WHOLE-KERNEL CORN,
DRAINED

½ CUP PACKED FRESH CILANTRO LEAVES

4 (10-INCH) LOW-FAT FLOUR TORTILLAS

6 OUNCES SHREDDED REDUCED-FAT
MONTEREY JACK CHEESE (1½ CUPS)

REDUCED-FAT SOUR CREAM (OPTIONAL)

1 Preheat oven to 500°F. Spray 15½" by 10½" jelly-roll pan with nonstick
cooking spray.

2 In small bowl, mix salsa and tomato sauce. In medium bowl, mix black
beans, corn, and cilantro.

3 Place 1 tortilla in jelly-roll pan. Spread one-third of salsa mixture over
tortilla. Top with one-third of bean mixture and one-third of cheese. Repeat
layering two more times, ending with last tortilla. Bake pie until cheese
melts and filling is hot, 10 to 12 minutes. Serve with sour cream, if you like.

EACH SERVING: ABOUT 440 CALORIES | 25G PROTEIN | 65G CARBOHYDRATE | 11G TOTAL FAT
(5G SATURATED) | 13G FIBER | 30MG CHOLESTEROL | 820MG SODIUM

BLACK BEAN AND AVOCADO SALAD WITH CILANTRO DRESSING

This main-dish salad is a satisfying combination of summer veggies, romaine lettuce, and black beans tossed with a creamy cilantro-lime dressing.

TOTAL TIME: 30 MINUTES

MAKES: 4 SERVINGS

2   LIMES

¼   CUP LIGHT MAYONNAISE

½   CUP PACKED FRESH CILANTRO LEAVES

2   TABLESPOONS REDUCED-FAT SOUR CREAM

½   TEASPOON GROUND CUMIN

¼   TEASPOON SUGAR

⅛   TEASPOON SALT

⅛   TEASPOON COARSELY GROUND BLACK PEPPER

1   SMALL HEAD ROMAINE LETTUCE (1 POUND), CUT INTO ¾-INCH PIECES (8 CUPS)

2   MEDIUM TOMATOES, CUT INTO ½-INCH PIECES

2   KIRBY CUCUMBERS (4 OUNCES EACH), NOT PEELED, EACH CUT LENGTHWISE INTO QUARTERS, THEN CROSSWISE INTO ¼-INCH PIECES

1   RIPE AVOCADO, PITTED, PEELED, AND CUT INTO ½-INCH PIECES

1   CAN (15 TO 19 OUNCES) BLACK BEANS, RINSED AND DRAINED

1   From limes, grate ½ teaspoon peel and squeeze 3 tablespoons juice. In blender, puree lime peel and juice, mayonnaise, cilantro, sour cream, cumin, sugar, salt, and pepper until smooth, occasionally scraping down sides of blender. Cover and refrigerate dressing if not using right away. Makes about ½ cup.

2   In large serving bowl, toss lettuce, tomatoes, cucumbers, avocado, and beans with dressing until well coated. Serve as soon as possible so that the avocado has no time to discolor.

EACH SERVING: ABOUT 230 CALORIES | 9G PROTEIN | 34G CARBOHYDRATE | 10G TOTAL FAT (2G SATURATED) | 12G FIBER | 3MG CHOLESTEROL | 520MG SODIUM

5 IDEAS FOR...BLACK BEANS

Low in fat, high in protein, and cholesterol free, black beans are a healthy basis for a quick, delicious meal. In all of these recipes, begin by rinsing and draining 1 to 2 cans of beans (each 15 to 19 ounces).

Black Bean Dip: In food processor, puree 1 can beans with 1 tablespoon fresh lime juice, 1 teaspoon freshly grated lime peel, and 2 teaspoons chipotle pepper sauce. Transfer to small bowl and stir in ¼ cup chopped cilantro leaves and 2 seeded, chopped plum tomatoes. Makes about 2 cups. (For a healthier alternative to tortilla chips, try carrot sticks, red pepper strips, or jicama slices.)

Black Bean Salad: In medium bowl, combine 1 can beans, 1 chopped red pepper, 1 can (15¼ ounces) drained corn kernels, ⅓ cup chopped cilantro leaves, and 2 tablespoons ranch dressing. Makes about 3½ cups.

Black Bean Soup: In large nonstick saucepan, cook 1 cup fresh salsa and a pinch of allspice over medium heat for 3 minutes. Stir in 2 cans beans and 3 cups low-sodium vegetable broth; heat to boiling over high heat. Reduce heat and simmer 10 minutes. Use immersion blender or potato masher to coarsely mash beans. Makes 6 servings.

Avocado and Black Bean Quesadillas: Divide 4 tablespoons salsa, 1 cup shredded pepper Jack cheese, beans, and 1 avocado among 4 burrito-size tortillas, placing fillings on one half of tortilla only. Fold tortilla over filling; press to flatten slightly. Heat 12-inch skillet on medium; add 2 quesadillas. Cook 8 minutes or until golden on both sides. Repeat. Serve with additional salsa. Makes 4 servings.

Black Bean Sauté: In nonstick skillet, brown 1 chopped small onion in 1 teaspoon olive oil. Stir in 1 clove garlic, crushed with press, and cook 1 minute. Stir in 1 can beans and heat through. Remove from heat and stir in 1 to 2 tablespoons chopped pickled jalapeño chiles. Makes about 1¾ cups. Serve over rice, if you like.

RED LENTIL AND VEGETABLE SOUP

STOVE This meal-in-a-bowl brims with fill-you-up soluble fiber, thanks to the lentils. Translation: It may help keep your weight down and helps lower total and "bad" LDL cholesterol. The lentils, spinach, and tomatoes, all rich in potassium, work to keep blood pressure in check, too.

ACTIVE TIME: 20 MINUTES · **TOTAL TIME:** 30 MINUTES

MAKES: 4 SERVINGS

1 TABLESPOON OLIVE OIL

4 MEDIUM CARROTS, PEELED AND CHOPPED

1 SMALL ONION, CHOPPED

1 TEASPOON GROUND CUMIN

1 CAN (14 TO 15 OUNCES) DICED TOMATOES

1 CUP RED LENTILS, RINSED AND PICKED THROUGH

1 CAN (14 TO 15 OUNCES) VEGETABLE BROTH

2 CUPS WATER

¼ TEASPOON SALT

⅛ TEASPOON GROUND BLACK PEPPER

1 BAG (5 OUNCES) BABY SPINACH

1 In 4-quart saucepan, heat oil over medium heat until hot. Add carrots and onion, and cook until tender and lightly browned, 6 to 8 minutes. Stir in cumin; cook 1 minute.

2 Add tomatoes with their juice, lentils, broth, water, salt, and pepper; cover and heat to boiling over high heat. Reduce heat to low; cover and simmer until lentils are tender, 8 to 10 minutes.

3 Just before serving, stir in spinach.

EACH SERVING: ABOUT 265 CALORIES | 16G PROTEIN | 41G CARBOHYDRATE | 5G TOTAL FAT (1G SATURATED) | 13G FIBER | 0MG CHOLESTEROL | 645MG SODIUM

MIXED VEGETABLE CURRY

STOVE Korma is a mild, creamy yogurt-based sauce; jalfrezi is tomato-based. You can find Indian simmer sauces in specialty food stores as well as in the Asian foods section of many larger supermarkets. To create a surprising, colorful mix—the easy way—use packages of fresh precut produce. Serve over fragrant basmati rice.

ACTIVE TIME: 10 MINUTES · TOTAL TIME: 15 MINUTES

MAKES: 4 SERVINGS

1 PACKAGE (16 OUNCES) MIXED FRESH VEGETABLES FOR STIR-FRY

1 BUNCH GREEN ONIONS, CUT INTO 2-INCH PIECES

½ CUP COLD WATER

1 CAN (15 TO 19 OUNCES) GARBANZO BEANS, RINSED AND DRAINED

1 JAR (15 OUNCES) INDIAN KORMA SAUCE OR JALFREZI RED PEPPER SAUCE, OR ONE 10-OUNCE CAN SAUCE PLUS ½ CUP WATER

1 CUP LOOSELY PACKED FRESH CILANTRO LEAVES

1 In nonstick 12-inch skillet, combine mixed vegetables and green onions; stir in water. Cover skillet and cook over medium-high heat until vegetables are tender-crisp, about 5 minutes, stirring occasionally.

2 Stir garbanzo beans and chosen sauce into vegetable mixture in skillet. Cover and heat to boiling, stirring occasionally.

3 Remove skillet from heat; stir in cilantro leaves to serve.

EACH SERVING: ABOUT 360 CALORIES | 12G PROTEIN | 57G CARBOHYDRATE | 10G TOTAL FAT (5G SATURATED) | 12G FIBER | 2MG CHOLESTEROL | 730MG SODIUM

SOUTHWESTERN BLACK-BEAN BURGERS

GRILL For a **super-easy bonus weeknight meal, make a double batch** of these burgers and freeze the extras. Then all you need to do is defrost them for 10 minutes and grill until heated through, about 12 minutes, turning once.

ACTIVE TIME: 15 MINUTES · **TOTAL TIME:** 20 MINUTES

MAKES: 4 BURGERS

---

1   CAN (15 TO 19 OUNCES) BLACK BEANS, RINSED AND DRAINED

2   TABLESPOONS LIGHT MAYONNAISE

¼   CUP LOOSELY PACKED FRESH CILANTRO LEAVES, CHOPPED

1   TABLESPOON PLAIN DRIED BREAD CRUMBS

½   TEASPOON GROUND CUMIN

½   TEASPOON HOT PEPPER SAUCE

NONSTICK COOKING SPRAY

1   CUP LOOSELY PACKED SLICED LETTUCE

4   (4-INCH) MINI WHOLE-WHEAT PITA BREADS, WARMED

½   CUP MILD SALSA

1   Prepare outdoor grill for direct grilling over medium heat.

2   In large bowl, with potato masher or fork, mash black beans with mayonnaise until almost smooth (some lumps of beans should remain). Stir in cilantro, bread crumbs, cumin, and pepper sauce until combined. With lightly floured hands, shape bean mixture into four 3-inch round patties. Spray both sides of each patty lightly with cooking spray.

3   Place burgers on hot grill rack over medium heat. Cook until lightly browned, about 6 minutes, turning once.

4   Arrange lettuce on pitas; top with burgers and salsa.

EACH SERVING: ABOUT 210 CALORIES | 13G PROTEIN | 42G CARBOHYDRATE | 3G TOTAL FAT (0G SATURATED) | 13G FIBER | 0MG CHOLESTEROL | 715MG SODIUM

LO MEIN WITH TOFU, SNOW PEAS, AND CARROTS

 STOVE

Packaged ramen noodles can be a great short-cut ingredient. Here they're combined with tofu, snow peas, carrots, and bean sprouts for a tasty homemade lo mein.

TOTAL TIME: 30 MINUTES

MAKES: 4 SERVINGS

---

2 PACKAGES (3 OUNCES EACH) ORIENTAL-FLAVOR RAMEN NOODLE SOUP MIX

2 TEASPOONS VEGETABLE OIL

1 PACKAGE (14 TO 15 OUNCES) EXTRA-FIRM TOFU, PATTED DRY AND CUT INTO ½-INCH PIECES

6 OUNCES SNOW PEAS, STRINGS REMOVED AND EACH CUT ON DIAGONAL IN HALF (2 CUPS)

3 GREEN ONIONS, CUT INTO 2-INCH PIECES

1½ CUPS SHREDDED CARROTS FROM 10-OUNCE PACKAGE

½ CUP BOTTLED STIR-FRY SAUCE

3 OUNCES FRESH BEAN SPROUTS (1 CUP), RINSED AND DRAINED

1 Set aside flavor packets from ramen noodles and cook in 4-quart saucepan, filled with *boiling water*, 2 minutes. Drain, reserving *¼ cup noodle water*.

2 Meanwhile, in nonstick 12-inch skillet, heat oil over medium heat until very hot. Add tofu and cook, stirring occasionally, until lightly browned, 5 to 6 minutes. Add snow peas and green onions to skillet; cook, stirring frequently, until vegetables are tender-crisp, 3 to 5 minutes. Stir in carrots, stir-fry sauce, and contents of 1 flavor packet to taste (depending on salt level of sauce); cook until carrots are tender, about 2 minutes. (Discard remaining flavor packet or save for another use.)

3 Set aside some bean sprouts for garnish. Add noodles, reserved noodle water, and remaining bean sprouts to skillet; cook, stirring, 1 minute. To serve, sprinkle with bean sprouts.

EACH SERVING: ABOUT 375 CALORIES | 18G PROTEIN | 47G CARBOHYDRATE | 12G TOTAL FAT (3G SATURATED) | 4G FIBER | 0MG CHOLESTEROL | 1,485MG SODIUM

THAI COCONUT SOUP

 The classic version of this soup contains sliced chicken. If you like, add 12 ounces thinly sliced chicken breast meat, cut into ½-inch slivers, to the pan instead of the tofu.

TOTAL TIME: 20 MINUTES

MAKES: 4 SERVINGS

2 SMALL CARROTS, EACH PEELED AND CUT CROSSWISE IN HALF	12 OUNCES FIRM TOFU, CUT INTO 1-INCH PIECES
½ MEDIUM RED PEPPER	2 CANS (14 TO 15 OUNCES EACH) VEGETABLE BROTH OR CHICKEN BROTH
1 CAN (14 OUNCES) LIGHT UNSWEETENED COCONUT MILK (NOT CREAM OF COCONUT), WELL STIRRED	
2 GARLIC CLOVES, CRUSHED WITH GARLIC PRESS	1 TABLESPOON REDUCED-SODIUM SOY SAUCE
2-INCH PIECE PEELED FRESH GINGER, CUT INTO 4 SLICES	1 TABLESPOON FRESH LIME JUICE
	1 CUP WATER
½ TEASPOON GROUND CORIANDER	2 GREEN ONIONS, SLICED
½ TEASPOON GROUND CUMIN	½ CUP CHOPPED FRESH CILANTRO LEAVES
¼ TEASPOON GROUND RED PEPPER (CAYENNE)	

1 With vegetable peeler, slice carrots and edge of red pepper lengthwise into thin strips; set aside.

2 In 5-quart Dutch oven, heat ½ cup coconut milk to boiling over medium heat. Add garlic, ginger, coriander, cumin, and ground red pepper and cook, stirring, 1 minute.

3 Increase heat to medium-high. Stir in tofu, broth, carrot strips, pepper strips, soy sauce, lime juice, water, and remaining coconut milk; heat just to simmering. Discard ginger. Just before serving, stir in green onions and cilantro.

EACH SERVING: ABOUT 210 CALORIES | 11G PROTEIN | 14G CARBOHYDRATE | 17G TOTAL FAT (6G SATURATED) | 4G FIBER | 0MG CHOLESTEROL | 1,060MG SODIUM

INDEX

Note: Page numbers in **bold** indicate recipe category lists.

PHOTOGRAPHY CREDITS

Antonis Achilleos: 37, 105, 131
James Baigrie: 21, 31, 40, 58, 89, 127, 147
Mary Ellen Bartley: 102, 132
Tara Donne: 26, 92
Philip Friedman/Studio D: 7
Frances Janisch: 50, 52, 68, 70
Brian Hagiwara: 6, 102, 111, 142, 151
iStock: pixhook, 8; Martin Kemp (utensils), VisualField (clock), 14
Rita Maas: 122
Kate Mathis: 128
Ngoc Minh Ngo: 47, 63, 97, 135
David Prince: 16, 32
Alan Richardson: 76, 83, 84, 136
Charles Schiller: 148
Kate Sears: 2, 106, 109, 121
Mark Thomas: 18
Cheryl Zibiski: 114

Front Cover: Alan Richardson
Spine: Antonis Achilleos
Back Cover (clockwise from top left): James Baigrie, Tara Donne, Rita Maas

METRIC EQUIVALENTS

The recipes that appear in this cookbook use the standard United States method for measuring liquid and dry or solid ingredients (teaspoons, tablespoons, and cups). The information on this chart is provided to help cooks outside the U.S. successfully use these recipes. All equivalents are approximate.

METRIC EQUIVALENTS FOR DIFFERENT TYPES OF INGREDIENTS

A standard cup measure of a dry or solid ingredient will vary in weight depending on the type of ingredient. A standard cup of liquid is the same volume for any type of liquid. Use the following chart when converting standard cup measures to grams (weight) or milliliters (volume).

Standard Cup	Fine Powder (e.g. flour)	Grain (e.g. rice)	Granular (e.g. sugar)	Liquid Solids (e.g. butter)	Liquid (e.g. milk)
1	140 g	150 g	190 g	200 g	240 ml
¾	105 g	113 g	143 g	150 g	180 ml
⅔	93 g	100 g	125 g	133 g	160 ml
½	70 g	75 g	95 g	100 g	120 ml
⅓	47 g	50 g	63 g	67 g	80 ml
¼	35 g	38 g	48 g	50 g	60 ml
⅛	18 g	19 g	24 g	25 g	30 ml

USEFUL EQUIVALENTS FOR LIQUID INGREDIENTS BY VOLUME

¼ tsp	=							1 ml
½ tsp	=							2 ml
1 tsp	=							5 ml
3 tsp	=	1 tbls	=			½ fl oz	=	15 ml
		2 tbls	=	⅛ cup	=	1 fl oz	=	30 ml
		4 tbls	=	¼ cup	=	2 fl oz	=	60 ml
		5⅓ tbls	=	⅓ cup	=	3 fl oz	=	80 ml
		8 tbls	=	½ cup	=	4 fl oz	=	120 ml
		10⅔ tbls	=	⅔ cup	=	5 fl oz	=	160 ml
		12 tbls	=	¾ cup	=	6 fl oz	=	180 ml
		16 tbls	=	1 cup	=	8 fl oz	=	240 ml
		1 pt	=	2 cups	=	16 fl oz	=	480 ml
		1 qt	=	4 cups	=	32 fl oz	=	960 ml
						33 fl oz	=	1000 ml = 1 L

USEFUL EQUIVALENTS FOR COOKING/OVEN TEMPERATURES

	Fahrenheit	Celsius	Gas Mark
Freeze Water	32° F	0° C	
Room Temperature	68° F	20° C	
Boil Water	212° F	100° C	
Bake	325° F	160° C	3
	350° F	180° C	4
	375° F	190° C	5
	400° F	200° C	6
	425° F	220° C	7
	450° F	230° C	8
Broil			Grill

USEFUL EQUIVALENTS FOR DRY INGREDIENTS BY WEIGHT

(To convert ounces to grams, multiply the number of ounces by 30.)

1 oz	=	¹⁄₁₆ lb	=	30 g
2 oz	=	¼ lb	=	120 g
4 oz	=	½ lb	=	240 g
8 oz	=	¾ lb	=	360 g
16 oz	=	1 lb	=	480 g

USEFUL EQUIVALENTS LENGTH

(To convert inches to centimeters, multiply the number of inches by 2.5.)

1 in =		2.5 cm
6 in = ½ ft =		15 cm
12 in = 1 ft =		30 cm
36 in = 3 ft = 1 yd	= 90 cm
40 in =		100 cm = 1 m

THE GOOD HOUSEKEEPING TRIPLE-TEST PROMISE

At *Good Housekeeping*, we want to make sure that every recipe we print works in any oven, with any brand of ingredient, no matter what. That's why, in our test kitchens at the **Good Housekeeping Research Institute,** we go all out: We test each recipe at least three times—and, often, several more times after that.

When a recipe is first developed, one member of our team prepares the dish and we judge it on these criteria: It must be **delicious, family-friendly, healthy,** and **easy to make.**

1. The recipe is then tested several more times to fine-tune the flavor and ease of preparation, always by the same team member, using the same equipment.

2. Next, another team member follows the recipe as written, **varying the brands of ingredients** and **kinds of equipment.** Even the types of stoves we use are changed.

3. A third team member repeats the whole process **using yet another set of equipment** and **alternative ingredients.**

By the time the recipes appear on these pages, they are guaranteed to work in any kitchen, including yours. WE PROMISE.